Built By The Owner's Design

The Positive Approach To Building Your Church God's Way

Danny Von Kanel

CSS Publishing Company, Inc., Lima, Ohio

BUILT BY THE OWNER'S DESIGN

Library of Congress Cataloging-in-Publication Data

Von Kanel, Danny, 1955-
    Built by the owner's design : the positive approach to building your church God's way / Danny Von Kanel.
        p. cm.
Includes bibliographical references.
    ISBN 0-7880-1952-X (pbk. : alk. paper)
    1. Church growth. I. Title.
    BV652.25 V66 2003
    254'.5—dc21

                                                                                2002013736

For more information about CSS Publishing Company resources, visit our website at www.csspub.com or e-mail us at custserv@csspub.com or call (800) 241-4056.

ISBN 0-7880-1952-X   PRINTED IN U.S.A.

*I dedicate this book
to the pastors around the world who
serve tenured churches in county seat towns.
Your churches because of tradition, bureaucracy, and
well-engrained procedures for doing church, are the most
difficult to grow. You are the true heroes of the faith in my
view. May this book bring encouragement.*

*I also dedicate this book
to church staff members who serve faithfully —
many times without public recognition of their contributions,
servant attitude, and unceasing effort. Your contribution
to church growth is to be commended.*

*Finally, I dedicate this book
to my wife Beverly, and sons, Allen and Brad,
for their support through 24 years of challenging,
learning, and yes ... growing ministry together.*

Table Of Contents

Acknowledgments

To my wife Beverly who has been a partner, friend, and encourager in my leadership in church work and my writing;

To my sons, Allen and Brad, who have expressed pride in their dad in ways that spurred my desire to write more;

To Dr. Randy Von Kanel, for his critiques and inspiration. My son, Allen, was right. Randy has to be one of the most loved preachers in the world. I guess that's why he's my hero in the ministry;

To Jackie Smith, for believing in my writing potential and for being the best secretary any minister could ever want;

To Nina Gant, Linda Tiller, and Sally McCoy for believing in me and always being a sounding board;

To Barbara A. Robidoux for her critiquing skills and unique way of encouraging me always to have hope in my writing potential;

To David Wachsman and Joyce Mabry for the critiques and kind words about my writings, even though I, a novice, was hearing words from two English professionals;

To Don M. Aycock, for taking the time to write a letter of advice aboard an airplane that gave me critical suggestions on improving my work ... and for returning my calls;

To many pastors who knowingly and unknowingly have contributed to my understanding of church growth — some have inspired me because they were good and some because they were poor;

To other pastors who contributed to the 3/3/50 Church Growth Survey used as research in this book, your contributions helped answer some of church growth's nagging questions;

To those congregations who have responded affirmatively to creative ways in doing ministry: First Baptist Church, Florala, Alabama; First Baptist Church, Purvis, Mississippi; First Baptist Church, Lucedale, Mississippi; First Baptist Church, Vandalia, Illinois; First Baptist Church, Macon, Mississippi; Liberty Baptist Church, Liberty, Mississippi; and Parkway Baptist Church, Pascagoula, Mississippi; and

To all writers in the area of church growth: though at times we have differed, you have been an inspiration to me: George Barna, C. Kirk Hadaway, Gene Mims, Henry Blackaby, Rick Warren, Thom S. Rainer, Waylon Moore, Bruce Wilkerson, John R. Cionca, Darrell Robinson, David Hocking, Donald McGavran, Jack Redford, Lyle Shaller, Paul Powell, Gary McIntosh, Glen Martin, Carl F. George, Paul Enns, and Robert Bailey.

Preface

Built By The Owner's Design has consumed my thinking over the past three years. Having come to the place of recognizing unaddressed areas in church growth dialogue, I sought to raise some serious questions that needed answers.

You will find some room for disagreement in these pages. As we look at the role of Sunday school, the subtle differences with the church growth movement, and the place of evangelism, please consider my rationale. The surveys, other research, and my experiences should weigh in on your conclusions.

You may wonder if I'm for or against the Church Growth Movement. Neither. I have found myself somewhere in the middle concerning this movement — rejecting some but accepting other tenets. I have specifically mentioned Rick Warren, pastor of the great Saddleback Church. Rick is doing a super work. He is a great pastor and man of God. But, being representative of the Church Growth Movement, I use him and his writings to focus our attention on some possible shortcomings and strengths of this movement.

Concerning my experiences, please keep in mind these were growth experiences in the program areas in which I was responsible. Sometimes they impacted the overall church growth, other times not.

Built By The Owner's Design will systematically lead to an examination of your church and to a tailored plan for growth. May God lead and bless on your journey.

Chapter One

Collapsing Platforms

In the early 1980s, I took a youth group to the Smoky Mountains of North Carolina for a retreat getaway. Hazy morning hikes up the mountain enticed many a curious camper to seek adventure through these excursions. One morning, five of our girls decided to take the challenge and join the trek. I was the only adult chaperone from our group lured by such exploration. So I went — a sponsor from our group was needed to accompany the girls.

Traveling with a party of 75, we ascended to the top. Then, to get a better view, we climbed onto a wooden platform attached to the side of the mountain. Suddenly, with sight and sound suspended in an eerie quietness, I saw people in front of me falling, as if in slow motion. The main support beam had snapped — broken in two jagged fragments. All 75 had fallen some ten feet to the side of the mountain.

Fortunately, amidst the dangling bodies, only a few scrapes and bruises were reported. When our guide regained control and had carefully led us off the now pendulous platform, I escorted my five hysterical girls down the mountainside. It was later determined that the framing of the platform had collapsed because the supporting structure was inadequate. The camp leadership had failed to inspect it.

Unfortunately, a similar scenario is the case for church growth. In an effort to get a good view of church growth, many churches climb onto established platforms — growth mechanisms that may be faulty in origin or lacking close examination — and then are shocked when these supposedly "secure" platforms suddenly collapse, leaving them to pick up the pieces. They come up lacking. "Only 10 to 15 percent of the Protestant churches in our nation today can be deemed highly effective."[1] Seventy percent are plateaued or declining.

Early in my ministry, efforts at growth were prone to structural failure. Pieces of debris lay scattered among fractured platforms. It wasn't a pretty sight. I soon learned, observed, and found practical ways to allow God to design his blueprint for my ministries. Built on secure church growth platforms, we were able to build in churches not known for growth — rural, county seat, First Baptist churches.

In south Alabama, God led us to engineer the largest attendance in twenty years. Another church I served in south Mississippi witnessed the largest involvement ever in church visitation, quadrupling its attendance in one night. The first eight months of ministry at a central Mississippi church, 36 teenagers made professions of faith, coming indirectly through the Sunday school program (more about this later). In order not to limit my growth experiences to the south, our church in the midwest touched our city when structural principles for growth were applied to a year-long interdenominational outreach project. All of these, as well as other church growth experiences, have come about as we have paid attention to how the church is built by the owner's (God's) design.

In these pages, I will offer you a viable alternative to growth — midway between the overzealous, church growth right and the decaying, critical left. The first two chapters address what's wrong with contemporary growth structures. Chapters 3 to 11 present a proven framework for growth. In chapter 12, I will lead you to tailor-make a growth plan.

Before I deal with the details of what we did and how you can find God's design for your church, it is important for us to look at how others are seeking to grow churches. We will examine why they are prone to failure — or at best, are faulty in design — particularly when applied to county seat or traditional churches.

So, what are these collapsing platforms of church growth?

Growth From A Program View

Growth based on starting new programs is failure prone. Strong statement, but don't misunderstand me. Programs in and of themselves are neither good nor bad. They are neutral. Life is breathed into them when they are initiated by the Holy Spirit's prompting. Too many churches are guilty of starting a new program the moment they sense a decline in attendance without seeking God's direction first. In fact, a church in decline would be wise to examine existing programs and eliminate the ones not bearing fruit. "Most churches have one or more programs that continue in spite of ample evidence that the program is innocuous at best and harmful at worst."[2] Growth based on starting new programs can collapse for the following reasons.

* Programs Rob Us Of Time

Start-up time for any new program of substance is lengthy, weighing us down with concerns of finances, personnel, and scheduling. With our laypeople's time already stretched to the limit by home, church, and community involvement, more time at church is the last thing they need or want. It is interesting to note that "when asked what qualities they would consider if they were to move to a new community and seek a church to attend, respondents in a recent survey prioritized 22 factors. The offering of different programs and ministries came in thirteenth place — falling into the 'of lesser importance' category."[3] Thus it seems that burdening members with another program will reap minimum results at best or resentment at worst unless an existing program is eliminated and the new one takes its place.

I was the world's worst when it came to starting new programs. It got to the place at one point in my ministry where people would say, "Oh, no, here comes Brother Danny with a new program." It's an adaptation of an old adage that says, "Programs don't grow churches; God does." How true. He only wants us to follow his design.

I can remember starting a new ministry I called our "Care Volunteers." These were laypeople I sought to train in counseling so they in turn could counsel others. The results, at first, were fair. The amount of paperwork and bureaucracy I created initially became a nightmare — with forever lost time — until we streamlined it.

In 1999/2000 I completed a Church Growth Survey of three denominations (Southern Baptist, United Methodist, and Presbyterian USA), three Baptist Associations (Lamar, Mississippi, and Covington) and fifty churches (henceforth the study is referred to as 3/3/50 throughout book). According to the survey some churches are over-structured, having a lot going on but producing little in results. Nine percent of Southern Baptist churches surveyed fit this description with 3 percent of those coming from growing churches. United Methodist churches surveyed showed none as being over-structured, while the Presbyterian USA displayed 22 percent.[4] A start-up ministry at this juncture would be devastating to these already over-burdened churches unless some unfruitful programs were discarded.

New programming may be a realistic option for the Southern Baptist churches (23 percent) who said they were under-structured — little happening with complaints of the church not offering enough. Eleven percent of the growing SBC churches said the same. Twenty percent fit this description among United Methodist while a whopping 44 percent of Presbyterian USA churches were characterized this way.

* Programs Are No Sure Ticket For Ministry Involvement Growth
A new program will not necessarily result in more congregants involved in ministry. Though new programs abound among Southern Baptist, United Methodist, and Presbyterian USA churches, pastors say only about four out of every ten adults who attend church services are actively involved in the church's ministry efforts. Just

one out of every three churches claims at least half of the congregation participates in active ministry.[5] 67.9 percent of people say they are "somewhat" or "not involved" with their faith. Though 19.7 percent have increased their involvement with their faith in the last ten years, 37 percent have decreased.[6] The more likely possibility when a new program is added is that members will either quit or involve themselves to the point of exhaustion and burnout.

I fit the latter early on in my ministry. So busy and so tired ... with little fruit to show for my efforts. As a matter of fact, I soon found that the busier you tried to keep your people, the more they resented you as a leader. Adding new programs while keeping ailing old ones will reap the opposite of more people being involved. I know. I tried.

My "FamiCare" program (that is how I spelled it — give me credit for originality) was a case in point. Its purpose was to involve parents, youth, and workers with youth in meaningful dialogue. It didn't. Those who did come resented getting out on another night of the week, except for my die-hard workers. They were too exhausted to know how they felt. One parent summed it up this way: "You know, here I am trying to spend time with my family at home and you have us at church again. Are we here for the sake of our families or for the sake of your program?" We lost this family.

* *Programs Can Replace Evangelism*

The average church member will readily substitute a new program for involvement in evangelistic outreach. They will do it and rationalize, "This is my service to the Lord and I don't have to share my faith; let others witness." If anything, church programming should free people to live out their faith, not provide an excuse for avoiding responsibilities.

In our 3/3/50 survey data, 31 percent of the Southern Baptist churches were said to be structured wrong, meaning they were programmatic but not evangelistic. Even among the growing churches (57 percent), according to the pastors, 17 percent also said they were structured wrong. Among United Methodist, 20 percent weighed heavy to the program side while 22 percent of Presbyterian USA churches fit this description. An interesting note here is that while more Southern Baptist Convention pastors view their ministries as being structured wrong as compared to United Methodist and Presbyterians USA, statistically speaking, they see themselves as more evangelistic.

George Barna tells us that "Jesus did not minister through programs. The early church did not appoint program managers. The Bible never exhorts us to create new programs."[7] To view church growth through program eyes is to lose time, creativity, and evangelism thrust, each a part of the New Testament expansion of God's church. Preoccupation with a program focus will bring this "collapsing platform" crashing down on our efforts at growth. More details will be given in chapter 7 on the three ways churches structure wrongly.

The church growth gamut is one of extremes. To some it's starting new programs without eliminating what's not working; to others it's holding on to the past. This latter extreme is also failure prone.

* Programs Entrenched In Tradition Stifle Creativity

How many church programs should be discontinued but are so entrenched by tradition and longevity that doing so would result in serious bloodletting and possibly our departure? "Every ministry program," says George Barna, "must constantly justify its existence through measures of life transformation because every program is considered expendable."[8] Oftentimes, creative solutions to existing church growth concerns are put aside to accommodate these monolithic, death-defying programs. They make starting a new one like asking someone to run over us with his car after he has already left tire tracks on our backs.

Pastor Jack found that out the hard way. Any reasonable person could see that the church discipleship program was struggling on Sunday nights — having done so for fifty years. All efforts to breathe life into it met with dismal results. So he set out to change it.

Jack proposed a series of short-term classes taught by different leaders. All the preparations seemed to be going well until the next deacons' meeting. Bill, the chairman, spoke up. "I don't feel we need to change our Sunday night program," he announced. "It has done well through the years, so why change it? If it's not working now, it's not the program! We need better leadership. Pastor, you can handle that. Don't you agree, fellows?" Before Jack could say anything, the other deacons expressed their agreement with Bill and, to his dismay, Jack found himself facing another tough year of a program he could not kill.

I can sympathize with Jack. My early years were spent capitulating and avoiding the difficult task of putting to rest dead programs because of the powers that be. My creativity was put on hold and the church was robbed of future blessings.

Growth From An Evangelistic View

Evangelism is synonymous with a growing church. To believe otherwise is to reject the Great Commission and all New Testament writings on the subject. Yet, it is shortsighted to ignore the other biblical mandates of discipleship and the social gospel.

At the turn of the century, "Evangelicals began to build defenses against the social gospel. In doing so, evangelicalism was rightly affirming the importance of evangelism but wrongly avoiding any recognition of other ministries as being a part of mission."[9] Though a shift to include both was explicitly stated at the International Congress on World Evangelization in 1974, it has not met wide acceptance in many areas of the evangelical community. This myopic platform for church growth leaves much to be desired in its focus, depth, and practice.

When our evangelism becomes number conscious with resulting shallow followers who are only good at talking the mandate, the end result is less than desired. Let's see why.

* Number Conscious Instead Of People Focused

This allegation has been around as long as the church growth movement. Its characterization, though untrue of balanced ministries,[10] rings genuine when leveled at many churches whose sole emphasis is evangelism. "We may win this world but make few cross-bearing disciples."[11] According to Douglas Webster, "American Christianity is increasingly tolerant of any and all methods as long as they bring numerical results."[12] Down the road, such acceptance leaves casualties of false professions, disillusioned church members, and church leaders scratching their heads wondering what happened.

This was my concern when 36 teenagers made professions of faith in central Mississippi over an eight-month period. I thought, "Will these kids turn out to be cross-bearing disciples? Will their conversions be for real?" I will address this further; but for now, suffice it to say, most were.

A people-focused ministry is maintained when meeting needs is primary, when empathy skills are developed among leaders, and structure is in place to preserve a balanced ministry. One cannot closely examine each person's needs and still see people only as numbers. Empathy connects us. Feeling their pain or their lostness attaches our lives in ways no reference to numbers implies. Structure, as presented in the latter chapters, provides caution when the leaders approach playing the numbers game.

* Shallow Followers Instead Of A Deep Household Of Faith

The danger of overloading our ship with evangelistic cargo is to risk shipwreck when the pressures, trials, and difficulties of life come storming in, tossing overboard all whose shallow faith is not firmly anchored. Evangelism must be tied firmly to discipleship if new Christians are to weather what the world throws at them. The resulting household of faith is deep in its understanding, pushing its ensuing evangelism to be more authentic, passionate, and grounded in its encounters with the world system.

When asked, "Does your church take great care in making sure new converts understand the demands of discipleship?", 60 percent of Southern Baptists surveyed said yes, as did 77 percent percent of Presbyterian USA and 60 percent of United Methodist. Yet, when asked, "Does your church have a new members training class or some other system of orienting new members to your church?" only 28 percent of Southern Baptist, 66 percent Presbyterian, and 40 percent United Methodist said yes.[13] Traditionally, United Methodists and Presbyterians have been less focused on evangelism and more on discipleship, but even they fall short in what they say compared to what they are doing. Southern Baptists have been negligent for too long in this area.

The high Presbyterian percentage may be somewhat deceiving. "Recently, in 1998, 173 presbyteries rejected a proposed constitutional amendment that would have undermined standards of sexual behavior by church officers. Though it was defeated, 59 presbyteries voted for it."[14] It makes you wonder what kind of discipleship was being taught. Those presbyteries who voted for it paid a terrible price: "An 11 percent attrition rate."[15]

* Talking The Mandate Instead Of Living Out The Commission

"According to a recent survey, it requires 1,000 laypersons and six ministers one year to lead one person to Christ."[16] "Nine of ten pastors call their church evangelistic. However, less than one out of three church attendees has shared his/her faith in Christ with a non-Christian within the past twelve months."[17] "Only 43 percent of all Christians believe it is very important that non-Christians convert to Christianity."[18]

A *10-Year Southern Baptist Profile* of 180 Southern Baptist churches in five Baptist associations reveals the ratio of baptisms to resident membership is 37 to 1. 39.6 percent had an average to a very high ratio. The total SBC ratio is 39 to 1.[19] Why is that? Why does it take that many church members to win one person to Christ? Could it be that more real evangelism would take place if our people were grounded in discipleship while emphasizing the mandate to witness? Instead of talking about the need for more Christians actively sharing their faith, why not deepen their walk with the Lord, undergirding their understanding of what it means to live out the Great Commission? Doesn't it make more sense for 1,000 mature giants in the faith to share a witness than 1,000 shallow, immature saints, who neither want to, know how, nor understand why?

George Barna, in a recent study, discovered that "nearly half of all American adults believe that Jesus Christ made mistakes during his earthly ministry. An equal proportion believe that during his time on earth, Jesus committed sins! ... Realize that a substantial number of those are actively sharing their theology with unbelievers. In fact, we are discovering that a majority of the individuals who evangelize harbor some significantly errant theological stand."[20] The need to know the true Jesus is paramount before we let others rush off to share him.

Does that mean new Christians should not witness? No, but it does mean our emphasis on maturing them needs to be as great as our efforts to send them on their mission.

Growth From A Marketing View

The world system of doing business, from providing goods and services for the consumer to meeting goals and objectives of the producer, has made its way into the church. Though at one time such an approach would have been seen as heresy, today it is the "going thing" in church leadership circles. From conferences to a proliferation of books promoting its wares, churches have embraced its concepts. Yet, this platform for church growth has some cracks in its two main support beams. On careful examination, its tenets of identifying a target audience and meeting felt needs fall short of God's design.

* Targeting An Audience Implies Narrowing The Focus
Of The Great Commission

Going into *all* the world is our mandate. When we deliberately choose to reach out to a certain segment of society who act, think, spend, look, and live like we do, we are snubbing our noses at those who don't. "It may create a comfort zone for evangelism, but it may also limit our spiritual growth and dependence upon God."[21]

If, somehow, the targeting were evenly spread among all races and social classes, we might be able to rationalize that churches were being good stewards of their energies and resources. Unfortunately, the reality is that churches involved in marketing today are limiting who they outreach to, namely, white, middle-class, college-educated baby boomers.

One church member's perception sadly portrayed this truth when she said, "I don't see others like me joining our church. I'm poor and not as cultured. I'm not accepted and don't think I ever will be. Why would I want to worship here anymore?" She came to

20

this conclusion after watching a steady stream of others join our church. Distressingly, she was right.

Jesus never targeted a certain segment of society. He reached out to the rich and poor, social elite and the social outcast, the religious authorities and the pagan gentiles. Indeed, his commission says to go to all the world, not just to those who are like us.

* Meeting Felt Needs Implies That What People Feel And Their Needs Are Synonymous With Their Real Needs

In an age of materialism, self-centeredness, and individualism, focusing on the baby boomer's felt needs should cause one to shiver at what those needs might be. Shorter and positive sermons which steer clear of sin and money are capturing the pulpits. Longer and more demanding are the list of conveniences churchgoers want. Everything from greeters to child care to an array of support groups make up the list. As long as a church continues to pamper people by satisfying surface desires without also stressing community and individual goals of self-sacrifice, body life responsibilities, and personal piety, it may be full of satisfied customers but inward be as dead men's bones.

The truth is, what people want may or may not be what they need. A platform of growth based on meeting felt desires without balancing those with real needs will ultimately falter. No church can maintain its desire to do justice, love mercy, and walk humbly with its God when it's distracted by using its energies and resources to indulge the whims of a select target group whose desires and motivations run contrary or, at best, at a surface level. Reach the baby boomers? Sure! But do it without compromise. Fortify the felt need platform by tempering it with a dose of real-need awareness. Structuring to meet real needs avoids compromise. It's a platform for growth that won't collapse.

---

1. George Barna, *The Habits Of Highly Effective Evangelistic Churches* (Ventura, California: Regal Books, 1999), p. 18.

2. *Ibid.*, p. 22.

3. "Americans Describe Their Ideal Church," Barna Research Group, www.barna.org, October 7, 1998.

4. 3/3/50 Church Growth Survey, completed by author, of three denominations (Southern Baptist, United Methodist, and Presbyterian USA), three Baptist Associations (Lamar, Mississippi, and Covington), and 50 churches.

5. "An Inside Look At Today's Churches," Barna Research Group, www.barna.org, October 30, 1997.

6. "Precepts National Ethos Survey," www.perceptnet.com, 1998, 18,500 respondents.

7. Barna, *User Friendly Churches* (Ventura, California: Regal Books, 1991), pp. 42-43.

8. Barna, *The Habits Of Highly Effective Churches*, p. 64.

9. Thom S. Rainer, *The Book Of Church Growth* (Nashville, Tennessee: Broadman Press, 1993), p. 151.

10. Thom S. Rainer, *Effective Evangelistic Churches* (Nashville, Tennessee: Broadman and Holman), p. 135. Note: A recent study by C. Kirk Hadaway found that newly growing churches are more likely to be involved in community ministries than declining churches.

11. *Ibid.*, p. 91.

12. Douglas Webster, *Selling Jesus* (Downers Grove, Illinois: Intervarsity Press), p. 29.

13. 3/3/50 Church Growth Survey by author.

14. "Membership Losses Three Times Higher In Amendment A Presbyteries," John H. Adams, *The Presbyterian Layman*, September 3, 1998.

15. *Ibid.*

16. Lay Evangelism School, *WIN Teacher's Manual*, Baptist General Convention of Texas, Evangelism Division, n.d., p. 5.

17. "An Inside Look At Today's Churches," Barna Research Group, www.barna.org, October 30, 1997.

18. Newsweek Poll conducted by Princeton Survey Research Associates. December 10-12, 1998. 806 adults nationwide, including 674 Christians.

19. *10-Year Southern Baptist Profile* on churches in Mississippi Association, Mississippi; Lamar Association, Mississippi; Jackson Association, Mississippi; Kaskaskia Association, Illinois; and Covington Association, Alabama. The designations for rankings were as follows: very low, 1-17; low, 18-26; moderately low, 27-35; average, 36-44; moderately high, 45-53; high, 54-62; very high, 63 and above. The lower the ratio, the better a church does in evangelism. This analysis of data was completed by the author.

20. "Culture Watch — Which Jesus Do You Follow," George Barna, www.wheaton.edu, April 14, 1999.

21. Webster, *Selling Jesus*, p. 69.

Chapter Two

Miscalculated Overpasses

As a child in the mid-1960s, I vividly remember passing an overpass in the city of Houston, Texas, that was different from most. My older brother saw my curiosity and said, "That's a million dollar mistake." He went on to explain that the designers of this interstate miscalculated. The two sections coming from opposite directions were supposed to meet. They didn't. A concrete wall was a reminder to all who passed by that the framing of the overpass was structured wrong.

Often churches do the same thing. In an effort to facilitate church growth, they mistakenly seek to join programs, evangelism, and marketing to fixed traditions, programs, or secularizations. The intended purpose of overpassing obstacles to church growth while streamlining quickness to growth goals is nullified when they fail to hook up. Time lost restructuring is magnified further when the repairs made are less than desired. The subconscious concrete wall left in the minds of the congregation is a vivid reminder to be cautious, albeit stubborn, when other "growth overpasses" are proposed by enthusiastic church staff.

What are these miscalculated overpasses?

Joining Programs To Fixed Traditions

Recently, the staff of First Church, Anywhere U.S.A., wanted to establish a children's outreach program. The church was woefully lacking in children and needed a focus in this area. Traditionally, the church planned children's activities through an elected children's committee. The staff approached the committee and shared their desire to reach more children in the community, offering to schedule activities once every two months on Sunday morning following the morning service. The activities were to be highly publicized in the community, with an invitation for all who would to come. The staff stressed the Sunday scheduling, noting the traditional Saturday meetings seemed to hinder some of the children from coming back on Sunday. Sunday activities would be over at 1:30 p.m. and a promotional tie-in to Sunday school would be provided.

It didn't take long for the children's committee to convey their decision. They wanted activities for "their" children and were not interested in changing the time, frequency, or purpose for the activities planned. A sophisticated, prim, and proper mother of three, a pillar in the church, summed up the committee's feelings: "My children have to go to school with these other kids, but they don't have to go to church with them."

Such is the problem of joining new programs or altering existing ones in a climate of fixed tradition. "The goal of a tradition-driven church is simply to perpetuate the past. Change is always seen as negative, and stagnation is interpreted as stability."[1] A maintenance mode mentality, established bureaucracy, and a growth paralysis causes this miscalculated overpass.

New Programs Struggle To Function In The Maintenance Mode

One key criticism of the established traditional church is its maintenance mentality. So preoccupied with the past, remembering its glory days, leadership seems to concede an inevitable decline and have mentally chosen a reactive state of maintaining the *status quo*. In such an environment, any new program is viewed with suspicion and can face heated opposition. If a new program does get off the ground but fails to bring about promised growth,

26

the maintenance crowd may blame the continued decline on the new program.

Not only is the *status quo* flock enamored with the past, it is afraid of the future. New programs represent future direction. They signify change. This variation from the norm is a form of heresy to many of these non-moving spiritualists. "How dare they change the way we do church!" is the proclamation to their close-knit circle of friends. Though not known to the leadership, subtle undermining can take place with the intended purpose being the failure of the new program.

John desired his deacons to be a servant body. Instead, they functioned as a deacon board. John abruptly began this change by announcing to his deacons they would soon begin the "Deacon Family Ministry" plan. Assigning individual families to deacons came easy. After months of reports at deacon meetings, John realized the men were not keeping up with their families. Upon asking his deacon chairman what was going on, the man replied, "Pastor, our board had no intention of doing your plan. We have never done this before and no one wanted to tell you we wouldn't do it."

* New Programs Struggle To Find Acceptance
In An Unchanging Bureaucracy

The first hurdle any new program faces is the acceptance by the powers that be. Most traditional churches have had years to build up complex rules and guidelines, many of which take the would-be program starter to numerous committees and department heads. Each is capable of becoming the wrecking crew, sabotaging the ministry before it gets off the ground.

This bureaucratic red tape is enough to discourage any entrepreneur in ministry. To go through such headaches only to have the plan rejected is more than most idealistic idea initiators can handle. More futuristic leadership is lost through this form of rejection than the church knows.

The older the church the more red tape ministers must confront. The more a church is committee-run, the more bureaucracy. New ideas can fly but pastors must be prepared to take it slow and easy.

27

My arrival in south Mississippi presented me with a prayer ministry that had dwindled from its former glory. Hearing stories of its past, I felt led to take the prayer ministry to new heights. Ultimately, the ministry would have forty volunteers, twenty alternates, eight to ten home pray-ers, a telephone, and an answering machine.

The church was somewhat familiar with an ongoing prayer ministry, but the direct telephone line and answering machine was another story. Taking our time, we implemented the "40-Hour Ministry" and waited ... and waited. Two years passed with faithful volunteers carrying on the ministry. The time was then ripe for a direct telephone line and answering machine. To my pastor, prayer ministry coordinator, deacon body, finance committee, and ultimately, the church, the new additions were presented. They found acceptance.

Had I presented the new additions upon arriving, they would never have found agreement. The unchanging bureaucracy would have struggled with embracing these new additions to an old program.

Joining Evangelism To Fixed Programs

Concord Baptist recently experienced revival. As a result of this spiritual awakening, the church wanted to renew its efforts to be more evangelistic. Having always heard that the Sunday school was the evangelistic arm of the church, and in some it was, they proceeded to promote the sharing of one's faith through the Sunday school. In three months' time, the evangelistic zeal had diminished with little fruit to show for it.

What happened? Concord had joined its evangelistic effort with what they perceived as a fixed program, in this case, Sunday school, instead of seeing Sunday school as evangelism. What the church failed to realize was that it had been in existence for over 100 years and had never carried out the task of evangelism through the Sunday school. Evangelism gets side-stepped, loses legitimacy, and starts with little momentum when it is joined to a fixed program.

*Evangelism Gets Side-Stepped When It Competes
With The Established Norm*

In declining churches, Sunday school's primary function is Bible study. Music Ministry's fundamental task in these same churches is praise and worship. They say, to insert in either the mandate of evangelism is to place an unnecessary and unproductive competition on each.

My experience has been that Sunday school does not reap an evangelistic windfall when viewed as a program. For example, the 36 professions of faith in central Mississippi occurred outside but was impacted by the Sunday school as ministry integrated. Six came at a WOW (Win Our World) weekend, six at a Christian alternative to Halloween called "The Judgment House," six at a youth camp, and the other eighteen from group members bringing their friends to Christ.

Music Ministry is used by many in event evangelism. But "no single methodology engendered as high a level of negative responses as did event evangelism." 68 percent of the respondents said, rather adamantly, that event evangelism was of no value in their church's evangelistic ministry. A pastor in Missouri commented, "We were extremely excited when nearly 200 unchurched persons showed up for one of our three days of Christmas celebrations." He continued, "And we were even more positive when 23 persons indicated on a response card they had accepted Jesus. We continued to have those types of responses for three years. But as we were planning our fourth year, I asked our minister of music to find out how many of the nearly eighty decisions in three years resulted in baptisms and integration in the church. Much to my disappointment and surprise, he could not name one."[2]

Generally, unless ministry integrated the task with the greatest understanding in people's minds will win out over its competition when implementing a new and foreign attachment to its purpose. In effect, it gets side-stepped.

Can Bible study result in people being committed to being more evangelistic? Yes, and it should. But here we are talking about program and not lifestyle. As we lead others to study the Bible, a natural outgrowth of our teaching is to encourage and nurture the sharing of what Christ has done in our lives and through the Holy Scriptures. But, the practicality of doing evangelism while placed inside an established "program" forces one program to receive the necessary focus while side-stepping the other. It's a competition that won't work.

Evangelism Loses Legitimacy When It Fails
To Produce In A Fixed Program

Any program over time must show fruit — fulfill its purpose — if it is to continue as a viable ministry. Because evangelism gets side-stepped when tied to an existing ministry, the actual number of professions of faith is minuscule. This poor showing can only lead to a loss of legitimacy in people's eyes.

In our 3/3/50 data of Southern Baptist churches we asked, "On a scale of 1-10, with 10 being the highest, how evangelistic do you see your church?" Of all the churches, the scale averaged at 3.7. In growing SBC churches, it was 5.7. In Presbyterian churches surveyed, it was 3.5 overall with 5.0 among growing churches. United Methodist churches saw themselves collectively as 5.1 on a 10-point scale with growing churches coming in at 5.7. The ten-year SBC profile disclosed that only 15.2 percent of the 180 churches reporting had a very low (1 to 1 through 17 to 1) ratio of baptisms to membership.[3]

When you compare this relatively poor perception of evangelism to areas of church life in which each looked for growth to occur, you can see where many churches have joined evangelism to a fixed program with less than average the result. 41 percent of SBC churches surveyed looked for growth to occur through the Sunday school. Presbyterians registered 20 percent through the Sunday school with an additional 30 percent through other fixed programs (kindergarten, small groups, playschool). Forty percent of the United Methodists looked for growth also through the Sunday school.

Such expectations for growth compared to how they perceive they are doing evangelism is reason enough to suspect tying evangelism to existing programs. Evangelism must not be tied to anything but exist as is: for example, Sunday school equals evangelism.

30

Both the United Methodist and Presbyterians USA national denominations have seen drastic declines while the Southern Baptist Convention has seen only modest gains, while recently seeing its first decline since 1926.[4]

Evangelism Starts With Little Momentum When Placed Inside A Long Existed Ministry

Ministries must have momentum if they are to involve people in their mission. Some have momentum just in their titles alone (for example: True Love Waits, Samaritan's Purse, and Evangelism Explosion). Still others gain this thrust from a charismatic leader (for example: Billy Graham Evangelistic Association and James Dobson's *Focus On The Family*). Most churches do not have the luxury of a known ministry title or of a charismatic personality to which to tie their evangelistic efforts. Even if they did, the end result would be less than expected unless the ministry name or dynamic leader epitomized a clear focus in evangelism.

The WOW (Win Our World) weekend was so successful because its only focus was evangelism. It had no other assigned task. Our youth knew exactly why they were participating — to be trained and led to witness.

Churches tend to place evangelistic outreach inside long-existing ministries. As in titles and personalities, if the ministry fails to grasp the essence of evangelism firmly, it will start with little momentum as it tries to carry out this important task. Sunday school should bring to mind evangelism. Evangelism placed inside Sunday school, unless given priority focus, will struggle to gain energy needed to accomplish its task — to push it towards greater numbers of souls being won to Christ.

Evangelism joined to fixed programs gets side-stepped when it must compete with the established norm. The norm must become evangelistic. The program loses legitimacy when it fails to produce and starts with little momentum when placed inside long-entrenched programs. It's a growth overpass that will never join up with optimal results.

Joining Marketing To A Fixed Secularization

In an effort to break out of the stale, declining, and safely-ensconced world of the established church, many entrepreneurial leaders have chosen to apply the marketing techniques of Fifth Avenue. In doing so, they have invigorated many New Testament concepts others have lost in the bureaucracy of doing church: namely, emphasis on outreach and evangelism, exciting worship, and purposeful ministry.

Yet, in all their efforts, they have mistakenly, or sometimes knowingly, joined marketing to a fixed secularization of doing ministry. They dilute the gospel and divest themselves of some New Testament practices while embracing worldly methods. This miscalculated overpass to church growth supposes that if the church will embrace some secular ideas of doing business, it will prosper. It is a calculated risk that shouldn't be taken.

* Marketing Can Dilute The Gospel's Message
To Attract The Masses

A tension exists between contextualization and accommodation. Contextualization means that the church understands its community or context. Accommodation, on the other hand, means that the church has let the world dictate its standards and values. Church marketers are aware of this tension but may be guilty of fudging between the two when they choose sermon topics that appeal to the unsaved listener or make "doing church" easier so the masses will be attracted.

"American Christianity is increasingly tolerant of any and all methods as long as they bring numerical results. We don't hear people praising the Lord because millions of people watch the NFL Super Bowl, but if 5,000 people attend church it must be God's doing."[5] And thousands are coming. There is no denying it. Bill Hybel's Willow Creek Community Church with its 15,000 plus and Rick Warren's Saddleback Church of 10,000 and growing are the first in a wave of mega-churches sweeping our land. How are they doing it? Are the methods God-honoring?

In Rick Warren's best selling book, *The Purpose Driven Church*, he uses five chapters to discuss how his marketing Saddleback brought in the crowds. In a nutshell, Warren says to

* Attract people as Jesus did.
* Use worship as witness.
* Design a seeker-sensitive service.
* Select music to fit the majority preference of the community.
* Preach to the unchurched.

The purpose of this discussion is to address each of these five areas of the Saddleback Church. Indeed, most are worthy of consideration. Saddleback has and is reaching people in a godly manner. My intent is to show how collectively they should be taken with caution because of their tendency to go too far with application.

No one can deny our need to attract people as Jesus did: to be loving of unbelievers, accepting without approving, and meeting people's needs. The question is: How far do we go? Do we love people enough to confront the sin in their lives? Do we continue to accept them even though they are not married and living together — with no end in sight of their changing while attending our church? At what point do we say, "Go and sin no more"? Does meeting people's needs require us to embrace any method? Jesus and the early church didn't. Neither does Saddleback. Neither should we.

The assertion that we use worship as witness questions the conviction that "only believers can worship God."[6] A person outside of Christ does not understand Christian worship. To bring it down totally to a seeker's level is somehow to make it less than Christian. In adopting the "come and see" approach as equal to the "go and tell" is to minimize the Great Commission. History tells us that most people are won to the Lord outside of the worship experience. What we see in our services is a public profession of that faith. Dual emphasis on coming and going has lulled believers into adopting the come approach, for it is the easiest of the two. For they say, "As long as our church is having people come to the seeker service, why should I go and tell?"

The Christian Church has always provided seeker-sensitive worship. But seeker-sensitive and seeker, as promoted by many others, is different. The traditional seeker service is sensitive to non-believers in a worship service, but the service itself is for followers of the living Christ. "We asked the leaders of 576 churches, 'Is a seeker service a factor in your church's evangelistic effectiveness?' A resounding 60 percent responded no."[7]

As a church musician, Warren has a valid point. People will go to the church where the musical taste is their preference. Church music of every generation has had to fight its battles. Today, the battle is between traditional and praise and worship. The hymns we sing today were once considered heresy, replacing psalmody. Those who argue for the "right" church music will, on close examination, mean what they personally like singing. However, a balance needs to be maintained between the majority preference and the minority taste of your members.

It is interesting to note that "of 22 factors tested (as to why people choose to attend a certain church), six proved to be of great importance, three others were of moderate importance, and the remaining thirteen were of lesser importance. Music was one of the bottom thirteen."[8]

Preaching to the unchurched is possible without diluting the message. Plan your titles to appeal to the unchurched and eliminate church language. Unfortunately, very few possess this capability. If the passion of our people is to reach the lost, preaching methods and models will matter little in our efforts. A worshiping church with solid biblical preaching will be electrified to go and tell, resulting in decisions for Christ outside the worship arena, but made public when God's people gather. Message dilution is less likely when we stick to preaching to the church, empowering it to take the gospel to the lost.

Recently, my present pastor electrified our people. He challenged us to take the gospel to everyone in a five-mile radius of our church. Using the G.R.O.W. program (a single-focus outreach program, I might add), our people accepted the task. It was a thrilling sight to see a different team out visiting, writing letters, and calling each week. His message had empowered us.

Marketing Can Divest Itself Of New Testament
Practices While Embracing Worldly Methods

The gospel through the ages has been for everyone. To target a particular audience implies, "You are not right for us. Go somewhere else if you want to go to church." As stated earlier, churches embracing marketing have seemingly targeted white, educated baby boomers. Doing so runs smack into the mandate of the Great Commission.

Church marketers have made strategizing a fine art. Reading their program offerings reminds one of a social agency or an entertainment club. Lost in their planning is the validity of the method. The biblical model enables the method the early church used — going out by twos. Reliance upon people coming instead of the church going — offering programs to meet felt needs instead of going to meet real needs — is a sure way to secure shallow followers. The demands Jesus makes of "dying to self" and "taking up your cross and follow me" will lead such "believers" to reject him, if the cares, riches, and pleasures of this world don't do it first.

"A church could master the art of marketing but neglect faithfulness, justice, and mercy. The successful church may be more entertaining than edifying and more exciting than holy."[9] A danger exists in going astray of the biblical model when we get so wrapped up in doing stuff — programs, strategies, and activities — in an attempt to attract an audience. The intangibles that matter are lost. Churches that have totally embraced marketing concepts (*total* being the key word) on the surface appear to have mastered the New Testament design. When you pull away their marketing veneer though, you may see a church that has neglected the deep intangibles of our faith. Aspects of marketing, yes. Total embracing, no!

When marketing is used to join fixed secularization's way of doing church, a watered-down gospel is possible and, in most cases, probable. The only churches I have seen that have managed to avoid this effect have been those (to be examined later) who have *not* embraced all of the elements of marketing and have maintained a structured balance in ministry. By doing so, they have avoided miscalculations and have established a true overpass to growth.

1. Rick Warren, *The Purpose Driven Church* (Grand Rapids, Michigan: Zondervan Publishing, 1994), p. 77.

2. Rainer, *Effective Evangelistic Churches*, Ten Surprises.

3. *10-Year Southern Baptist Profile* as given by SBC churches in five associations in Mississippi, Illinois, and Alabama. Data was analyzed by the author.

4. *Office Of The General Assembly*, John H. Adams, May 20, 1999, www.layman.org. Note: Presbyterian USA declined by 21,517 in 1998. The decline from 1967-1997 was more than 30,000 annually. Since the mid-1960s, the Presbyterian Church USA has lost more than a million members. *Survey Research Center*, www.icpsr.umich.edu/GSS report No. 26, by Tom W. Smith. Note: from 1960-1991, the religious preference for United Methodist went from 16.1 percent to 11.1 percent; Gallup, in same report, from 1967-1986 presents data of United Methodist preference from 14 percent to 9 percent. Baptist Press, *Mississippi Baptist Record*, April 29, 1999 issue. Note: 1998 is the first year since 1927 Southern Baptist have seen a decline in total membership. The decline was 162,158 or 1.02 percent.

5. Webster, *Selling Jesus*, p. 29.

6. Warren, *The Purpose Driven Church*, p. 239.

7. Rainer, *Effective Evangelistic Churches*.

8. "Americans Describe Their Ideal Church," Barna Research Group, www.barna.org, October 7, 1998.

9. *Ibid.*, p. 69.

Chapter Three

The New Testament Design

The early church must be the basis for our church growth design. Jesus died for the church. It behooves us to look at what his apostles were led to establish and how that is the basis for the rest of this book. As we have viewed growth through some collapsing platforms and seen the result of trying to join growth mechanisms to fixed programs, traditions, and secularizations, let's now take a look at what the early church says, if anything, about programs, evangelism, and marketing.

The Early Church And Programs

Webster defines "program" as "a plan of procedure." The word does not appear in Scripture, yet definite plans were made by the apostles. In Acts 2:45-47, it says: "And (they) sold their possessions and goods, and parted them to all men, as every man had need. And they continued daily with one accord in the temple, and breaking bread from house to house, did eat their meat with gladness and singleness of heart, praising God, and having favor with all the people. And the Lord added to the church daily such as should be saved."

A definite course of action was set in motion. They sold their possessions and distributed to them in need. This benevolent deed was the first program of the early church. Though not specifically stated, it implies that someone had to know who was needy and a way, a procedure, had to be implemented to get the goods to them.

Also implied is the procedural plan of how to continue now that Jesus was gone. At some point, they agreed (adopted a plan) to meet at the temple and observe communion in homes. This brings us to evangelism.

* Though Programs Can Replace Evangelism,
Here They Enhance It

Can you imagine what would happen if our lost world saw the church selling its possessions and giving to every man as he had need? Probably not much, until they saw us doing it in one accord and in singleness of heart. This action by the early church brought favor from the people. ("And the Lord added to the church daily such as should be saved.") When a church finds favor with the people, the fields are ripe for harvesting. Evangelism was enhanced as the early church structured itself to meet a real need and gave itself completely to be used of the Lord.

What took place at our church in central Mississippi defies explanation. The 36 teenagers received Christ amidst an overhanging presence which permeated every program. This spiritual dimension enhanced the likelihood lives would be changed. If a person was lost without Christ and in our circle, it was as if he had to get saved. The pure emotion and relative ease of these converts demonstrated our singleness of heart — and their finding favor.

* A New Program Can Bring Life When It
Replaces An Old Unproductive One

Scripture records for us in Acts 6:1-3, "And in those days, when the number of the disciples was multiplied, there arose a murmuring of Grecians against the Hebrews, because their widows were neglected in the daily ministration. Then the twelve called the multitude of the disciples unto them and said, 'It is not reason that we should leave the Word of God, and serve tables. Wherefore,

38

brethren, look out among you for seven men of honest report, full of the Holy Ghost and wisdom, whom ye may appoint over this business.' "

It seems that the old program the disciples had for looking after the widows of the Greeks and Hebrews was no longer working. The Grecians were murmuring against the Hebrews because their widows were being neglected. The disciples felt they could not preach the Word of God and wait on tables. Their plan of procedure was to find seven men to meet this need.

Sometimes programs must be started to fix something broken, as in this case. Notice, though, the former way of taking care of the widows was never mentioned. The disciples did not continue providing care for the widows along with these first deacons. They quit and started concentrating on preaching and teaching the Word.

At the south Mississippi church, our Discipleship Training program was broken. Always poorly attended, our people saw no value in long, boring classes. One of their reasons for staying away was the length of the commitment. In addition, they wanted more choices.

Kicking the change off with a Discipleship Training Fair while offering short-term classes, our people wholeheartedly responded. Our Sunday night program quadrupled over the course of the year.

The Early Church And Evangelism
The early church multiplied after Jesus' resurrection and ascension. With boldness the Word went out and brought forth fruit. Explosive, spirit-filled energy gripped those who heard the apostles, and resulted in multitudes coming to Christ. No more is this evident than in the lives of Paul and Peter. Paul, by his speech and life, exemplified the risen Christ. Peter gave rise to evangelism outside a fixed tradition.

* Talking Plus Living The Mandate Reaps Rewards
Paul and Barnabus had entered Antioch. They attended the synagogue on the Sabbath when Paul stood and preached boldly (Acts 13:14-41). After the Jews left, the Gentiles persuaded them to come back the next Sabbath. On their return, "almost the whole city"

(Acts 13:44) turned out to hear. Angered, the Jews began contradicting and blaspheming the apostles. And again Paul waxed bold, proclaiming the gospel to the Gentiles. "And when the Gentiles heard this, they were glad, and glorified the Word of the Lord; and as many as were ordained to eternal life believed. And the Word of the Lord was published throughout the region" (Acts 31:48-49).

Paul showed by his life and speech — proclaiming Jesus the Christ — that his faith was real. His language was the same to the religious leader and Gentile seeker alike. His faithful preaching of the Word with boldness reaped a harvest of souls. It also angered the religious elite who ran Paul and Barnabus out of town (v. 50). No sensitivity to the fears and hang-ups of unbelievers was evident in Paul's preaching at Corinth. In most places he went he reaped a double whammy — the reward of saved souls and the persecution of those he angered with his strong rhetoric.

When I served in the Midwest, I was provided with a unique opportunity to present the gospel. Framework Emphasis, a year-long interdenominational youth project I chaired, galvanized the community. Though strongly supported by sixteen churches of various faiths, two liberal churches, the school board, and the city council fought our efforts. But God helped us win the victory. The rewards were God's as lost souls were saved. The city was forever touched by the gospel.

* Evangelism Taken Out Of A Fixed Tradition Can Flourish

Peter, too, went against tradition when he took the gospel to Cornelius. The apostles and brethren who were in Judea heard how the Gentiles had received the Word of God and were contentious with Peter saying, "Thou wentest in to men uncircumcised, and didst eat with them" (Acts 11:3). Peter declared how God sent him to Cornelius and how the Holy Ghost had fallen on this Gentile and those with him just as he had with himself and the apostles. And "when they (the apostles and the brethren in Judea) heard these things, they held their peace, and glorified God saying, 'Then hath God also to the Gentiles granted repentance unto life' " (Acts 11:18).

Suppose that the apostles and brethren who were in Judea did not accept Peter's explanation for taking the gospel to the

Gentiles; suppose they stuck to their established tradition. The possibility would exist for you and me to be without the gospel today. Praise God that evangelism that day was birthed out of a fixed tradition and was able to flourish throughout the known world.

The same is true for us today. Areas of our ministries are based upon tradition. They have become so ingrained in the framework as to strangle evangelistic efforts. It's time to move on. A healthy defense of any move will meet with receptive ears if the leadership is attuned to God's anointing and His leading.

The Early Church And Marketing

"The early church and what?" you say! I know. It's a far stretch but consider with me some aspects of marketing the early church was doing and how they strengthened the gospel's delivery to attract the masses and widened the marketing focus of the Great Commission.

** Aspects Of Marketing Strengthens The Gospel's
Delivery To Attract The Masses*

Today's marketers can be commended for their conscious effort to meet needs. Unfortunately, as discussed earlier, they have mistakenly substituted felt needs for real needs. They use meeting felt needs as an attraction to get people to come to church. Peter and John met the real needs in the hearts of people so that "many of them which heard the Word believed and the number of men were about five thousand" (Acts 4:4).

If God can use "unlearned and ignorant" men (Acts 4:13) to entice people to come to Christ without tiptoeing around what they like and don't like, then it should motivate us to do the same. The masses are still attracted to unadulterated truth. The key is finding out the real needs of people and giving them God's truth as contained in Scripture.

** Imitating Ways Marketing Targets An Audience Widens
The Focus As The Great Commission Intended*

Had church marketing had its way with the church at Jerusalem, the gospel would have remained there. Gentiles were not the target audience. Christian Jews wanted to reach other Jews with the gospel message. The needs, wants, desires, and wishes of Gentiles would have been ignored.

The midwestern city was like most northern cities. The residents of the city said, "Have church, but do your religion thing in the walls of your building. Stay off the streets and out of the marketplace." Thank God we chose to follow God's blueprint. Though what we did was not without structural miscues, we followed God's lead. The focus of The Great Commission was widened because we chose to leave the comfort of our four-walled buildings and entered society's marketplace.

Today, our marketing brethren have done a good job in identifying who needs to be reached. Why can't these same techniques be used to widen our target, both to Jew and Gentile, rich and poor, so we will reach our whole community for Christ? Is it true that if you don't narrow your target audience you will have too wide a focus and will ultimately reach fewer? Tell that to our churches who have a multi-cultural make-up. They have decidedly left their comfort zone and have, as Jesus did, chosen to love all, regardless of creed or culture.

Sad to say, the number of churches who have chosen Jesus' cross-cultural way is few. "Half of our pastors (51 percent), claim that their church is multi-cultural, however, research shows that in more than 80 percent of the congregations in America, at least 90 percent of the congregants are of the same racial group."[1] Has anyone dared asked the question, "Is our lack of growth in any way connected to our refusal to embrace those from a different culture, thereby limiting God's blessing?"

Church marketers have targeted their audience geographically, demographically, culturally, and spiritually. We must do the same but to *all* audiences in our community. Once identified, the values, interests, hurts, and fears can spur us beyond the superficial felt needs to what's real. Meeting deep-seated real needs will bring anyone to church — even if your church's primary make-up is of congregants of a far different refinement. Can two or more cultures reside in the same place? Yes, indeed! Managing such diversity happens when a church is structured to meet equally the needs of each representative culture, much like the early church did when the Grecian and Hebrew widows were being neglected. Combined with a corporate focus on Jesus Christ, this intentional targeting of needs will result in church growth.

In the 3/3/50 Church Growth Survey, pastors were asked: "Can your church now, and has it in the past, been able to discern truth in times of crisis?" 74 percent of the Southern Baptist; 66 percent of the Presbyterian; and 40 percent of the United Methodists said yes.[2] We are at a crisis regarding growth in our churches. Most are plateaued and declining while others, though outwardly growing, are wholeheartedly embracing the church growth movement without a clue as to where it is taking them. If ever we needed to discern truth in this area, it is now. May the chapters that follow provide some truth as we attempt to build the Church by the Owner's design.

---

1. "An Inside Look At Today's Churches," Barna Research Group, www.barna.org, October 30, 1997.

2. 3/3/50 Church Growth Survey by author.

Chapter Four

The Building Of The House

The dilapidated, tattered hotel is no longer anchored to its pristine location in the city of Jackson, Mississippi. I was there as a teenager during its final days as a lodging provider and home for the Mississippi State Youth Congress. Our arrival, as a delegation from Pascagoula High School, Pascagoula, Mississippi, was evidence the towering and majestic landmark had seen better days — days in which throngs of teenagers did not roam and bring injury to its once elegant hallways. It was now a minuscule picture of its former beauty and grandeur.

Many churches, particularly the traditional ones, have been let go. Not so much in their physical facilities, though how they appear says much, but rather in the inner structures that nurtured new life and growth in their early years. They have lost their desire and energy for the process of growth. Though "Developing structure may be a boring or personally taxing adventure, ... it is one whose benefits justify involvement in the process."[1]

The evangelical community is frantically searching for this process, for how to bring life to old structures, to old ways of doing church so growth will occur. And they need to. "Somewhere between 65 and 85 percent of all Protestant congregations founded more than a decade ago are either shrinking in number or are on a plateau in size."[2] In their search for answers to growth, pastors and church boards are either willing to unquestionably embrace the church growth movement, with its inherent collapsing platforms or miscalculated overpasses, or beat to death programs that quit working years ago. The help that is available is more applicable to either the mega church or the new church. The established traditional churches, though the vast majority, are left to live out their days in decline until the Lord comes or until a wrecking crew brings them down. How can they grow amidst fixed traditions, debilitating bureaucracies, and love affairs with the *status quo*?

The answer lies in the very facility they meet in to worship, for building a growing church parallels the building of a church structure. They must go back to the day they were first built.

I sat in amazement as I watched the Methodist church behind our house begin a new addition to their church. Being all thumbs when it comes to woodworking, I was fascinated by the precision of the workmanship and the logical sequence of steps. First the foundation, then the structure, followed quickly by the walls and roof. As each was put in place, I remember thinking, "I wonder if these construction workers have any idea that building a church building or any construction is a lot like erecting a growing institution called the local church."

The building of the House of God is the product of a diverse group of gifts (sub-industries), with many individuals involved in the construction of a single body (structure), from the creating (manufacturing) of necessary components to the final living, growing organism (assembly).

In the church, the pastor and staff (Southern Baptist), superintendent or bishop (United Methodist), or elder board (Presbyterian) become the architect. The Owner (God) provides the direction through which the architects must follow his desires. These desires are then converted into a set of drawings and written specifications that are sent to the general contractors (church members with specific gifts to meet specifications).

46

Contractors ordinarily carry out their work under the observation of an architect who acts as an agent of the owner. God's people, in building and growing his church, must carry out their work, using their spiritual gifts, under the observation of the above mentioned church leaders who act as agents of God.

The first step — obtaining the right blueprint from the Owner — is the most important step of all. "Churches cannot waste time, energy, and effort," says Gene Mims, "doing things that are not a part of God's plan."[3]

At our church in south Mississippi, I found the music and education programs needing work. After a number of months of listening and learning as to what was working or not working, I brought our leadership together in a retreat setting to grab hold of God's blueprint. That retreat set the stage for what was to follow. The end result was our music ministry flourished from five music groups to twelve in a three-year period. We went from 180 involved to 320. As a bonus, our Discipleship Training prospered as it quadrupled in attendance.

In south Alabama, the room was electrified in another one of these blueprint-seeking sessions. The leadership grasped the potential for a series of "October Encounters." These special high attendance days had captured the hearts and minds of those present with a deep assurance that this was what God wanted. Leaving the room that night I knew we were in for a special treat from our Lord. And was I right! Every Sunday we went over our goal. In this sophisticated First Baptist Church, not known for applauding, the congregation broke out in applause as each Sunday's attendance was announced. This was the highest attendance, as one member told me, "In twenty plus years since I have been a member."

Establishing a living, growing church is at a pivotal point in its building when the architect (pastor, staff, bishop, or elder board) gets the requirements from the Owner (God). If the architects fail to consult the Owner, change the blueprint, or do their own thing, then the end result will not have the Owner's blessing.

It's interesting that in my 3/3/50 survey, 65 percent of Southern Baptist churches said they had no long range plan. Of those, 52 percent were from growing churches. Of the 34 percent who did have a plan, only 33 percent of those said it was written in the form of a vision for their church. Presbyterian USA churches had 22 percent with a long range plan in place while United Methodist registered 40 percent. It is clear from this data that seeking God's blueprint — his requirements for growth — is the step that is missing in many of our churches.

Not so for those that are growing. George Barna says, "My perception of the growing churches was that they were on a mission. They knew who they were, where they were headed, how they planned to get there, and why it was vital for them to do so."[4]

This blueprint or vision for each church is sometimes not clearly grasped by the leadership. It may require additional input. I'll never forget one perceptive music leader at a planning retreat who said, "What if God sent us all these musically-talented teenagers to play handbells? We could have a skill level grading of multiple groups." We agreed with this suggestion and the result was three youth handbell groups — beginner, intermediate, and advanced. Our handbell program was forever impacted by these groups.

George Barna tells us that "the purpose of gaining the perspective of outside counselors is not to allow them to determine or frame the vision. Rather, they can help you be as certain as possible that you have truly grasped the vision God has for you and have not succumbed to the desire to follow the ways that seem right to you alone."[5]

I am reminded of a pastor I served with who, years earlier, had purchased a house for $30,000 that was now being appraised for $118,000. His family had since grown up and this house was much too large for them to keep up. So, while his first home was being put up for sale, he announced to the church that God had led him to build a second house for $60,000. The problem came when the first house would not sell. And the pastor had to pay two house payments. He had turned down a $100,000 offer for the first house because it was appraised for more, so he was forced to go back to the church, this time to say he did not know God's will in the matter and needed church help.

Sometimes our best intentions seem right when it comes to building a home (physical construction) or a church (spiritual construction), but some timely advice can help us avoid mistakes and ultimately find God's will.

Before you begin to build a growing church, encourage the pastor and staff, superintendent or bishop, or elder board to get away for a few days. Seek God's face in prayer. "Find out what the Master is doing, then that is what you need to be doing."[6] Use church demographics, church surveys, prior church history, and God's Word to embrace God's blueprint for his church. Begin to develop habits that are strategic. "Habits that are not strategic have no place in ministry, they simply consume precious resources for no valid end,"[7] says Henry Blackaby.

As you seek God's face, remember three things. One, no two churches are exactly alike. Two, no two church growth frames will be precisely the same. Three, your plan must include the embracing of the Great Commission.

The Foundation

The Great Commission, Christ's final words to his disciples and the rallying cry of the godly through the ages, should be the foundational base in your construction. Jesus Christ becomes the foundation, the chief cornerstone. In fact, Psalm 27:1 says, "Unless the Lord builds the house, its builders labor in vain." Matthew 16:18 quotes Jesus as saying, "I will build my church."

As Christ becomes that base, your church will begin to embrace truth. George Barna tells us that "this will be a decade in which we must refocus our energies upon restoring our foundation. People who ascribe to or who evaluate Christianity cannot automatically be assumed to be on a solid foundation of truth."[8] When they are not on a solid foundation, they are unhealthy. "Church growth is the natural result of church health."[9]

A weak foundation of truth in our leaders and members limits growth, produces weakness, and leaves live weights that can cause our construction to crumble under the pressure. Rick Warren says that "your church's foundation will determine both its size and strength. You can never build larger than your foundation can handle."[10]

49

For our purposes, Jesus Christ becomes the foundation through the Great Commission in the phrase, "Lo, I am with you always." Every growth measure focused on Christ — acknowledging his presence in the process — will reap spiritual fruit.

Unfortunately, many of our county seat First churches have people in leadership who do not live the truth. My experience has included one in every First church. Their focus is not on Christ. Some of these people were strategic thinkers. But "It is possible to be intentional, strategic, and productive yet be outside the boundaries provided by Scripture."[11] And they were. In our church in south Mississippi, although they might have been an industry leader, lawyer, or doctor, when they were placed in a place of power, we had devastating consequences.

The way to deal with such lay leaders is to keep focusing on God's mandate, nurture spiritual growth in other leadership, and pray diligently for the errant leader by name. Ask God for a spiritual awakening in their souls. In time, they will lose their influence or fall because of moral failure. If not, recognize their contribution. Plug them into where they can do the least damage. Wait for God's direction in dealing with them. Always be willing to restore them when they return in repentance and faith.

In the Midwest, I had to deal with a difficult minister who fought us on every turn in our "Framework Emphasis"[12] interdenominational youth project. In light of his lifestyle and demeanor, one had to conclude his objections were not valid. They were a hindrance to the gospel. Prayer, confrontation, and exposing the truth were tools we used to deal with his attacks. Fortunately, the evangelical community rallied behind our efforts. Spiritual fruit was the result.

A natural outgrowth for this spiritual fruit gained from spiritual battles for truth is seen in how deeply Christ is magnified in worship and allowed to abide in the body through personal quiet times. "The more one is grounded in the deep things of God, the more it will overflow in worship and yield a desire to spend more time with God." Our central Mississippi church youth knew this foundational truth. Their foundational emphasis on having personal quiet times helped build a strong foundation where truth reigned.

In the construction industry, loads imposed on a building are classified as either dead or alive. The dead loads include the weight of the building itself and all the major items of fixed equipment. Live loads include wind pressure, seismic forces, and vibrations. Dead loads are constant. Live loads are temporary.

In the church, dead loads are the constant pressures placed on God's people. These continuous areas of stress are weekly meetings of worship and study, financial obligations, and ongoing staffing and maintenance. Later we will also see how the dead load of discipling relates to each area of structure. The temporary live loads come in the form of the winds of change, tragic deaths in the membership, inner church conflict, truthless leadership, and more. These loads can become unbearable for any church unless a firm foundation in Christ has been laid — where truth reigns and we understand that "Lo, I am with you always" (Matthew 28:20).

This fundamental structural base forces us to conclude that kingdom growth only happens when Jesus Christ is the foundation of the church. Even if dead and live loads were not present in church life, kingdom growth would be impossible without Christ as foundation.

A dead corpse does not feel pressure or pain; nor can it grow. It's important that you not automatically conclude that numerical growth is the same as kingdom growth, especially since "on the average, nearly half of the people who attend worship services at Protestant churches are not Christian."[13] Even more so, consider the Mormons. They are a growing religious group in number but not in truth. Kingdom growth will result in more people. But a greater quantity of members added to one's church does not instinctively mean kingdom growth is occurring.

To help you know if Christ is the foundation for your church, use the following evaluation as a tool.

Foundational Evaluation

1. The owner (God) has revealed his purpose and vision to the architects (pastor and staff, bishop, or elder board) of the church.
    _____ yes _____no

2. The contractors (church members) of our church know their spiritual gifts and are using them.
    _____ yes _____no

3. Christ is magnified and glorified in our worship services.
    _____ yes _____no

4. Fifty percent or more of the contractors (church members) have a daily personal quiet time. (Use markings on church envelope system to determine this percentage.)   _____ yes _____ no

5. The church can discern truth in times of crisis.
    _____ yes _____ no

6. Problems and decisions are addressed by asking, "What does Christ want us to do?"
    _____ yes _____ no

7. Spiritual growth is equal to or outpacing numerical growth. (A judgment call is made here based on your perceived understanding.)
    _____ yes _____ no

8. The church is experiencing numerical growth.
    _____ yes _____ no

9. Contractors (church members) are openly talking to their peers about matters of faith in the church and marketplace.
    _____ yes _____ no

10. The majority of contractors (church members) are making morality decisions and ethical decisions based on the truth of Scripture.

_____ yes _____ no

Use the following table to determine if Christ is the foundation of your church. Count the number of statements answered with a "yes."

Yes 1-3 times = Poor Foundation
Yes 4-7 times = Weak Foundation
Yes 8-10 times = Strong Foundation

Make a note of your score because we will be coming back later to address your church weaknesses in this area.

A home on Highway 11 coming out of Purvis, Mississippi, caught my eye — not for what I saw, but for what I didn't see. It was gone. On investigation I learned that the foundation had been faulty. The entire house had to be torn down and started over.

If the foundation of your church is faulty, don't tear it down. But do restore slowly, repairing its defects as you go. Recognize that houses function poorly with defective foundations and so do churches. Where the foundation is faulty, kingdom growth is impossible.

1. Barna, *The Habits Of Highly Effective Churches*, p. 58.

2. C. Kirk Hadaway, *Growing Off The Plateau* (Nashville, Tennessee: Broadman Press, 1989), p. 26.

3. Gene Mims, *Kingdom Principles For Church Growth* (Nashville, Tennessee: Broadman Press, 1994), p. 107.

4. Barna, *User Friendly Churches*, p. 186.

5. George Barna, *The Power Of Vision* (Ventura, California: Regal Books, 1992), p. 92.

6. Henry Blackaby, *Experiencing God* (Nashville, Tennessee: Lifeway Press, 1994), p. 18.

7. *Ibid.*, p. 23.

8. George Barna, *The Frog In The Kettle* (Ventura, California: Regal Books, 1990), p. 146.

9. Warren, *The Purpose Driven Church*, p. 17.

10. *Ibid.*, p. 143.

11. Barna, *The Habits Of Highly Effective Churches*, p. 23.

12. Framework Emphasis was a year long interdenominational youth project involving sixteen churches of all faiths from August, 1986 — May, 1987. The author was the founder and chairman of this project.

13. Barna, *The Habits Of Highly Effective Churches*, p. 93.

Chapter Five

The Erecting Of The Structure

Travels to Mobile, Alabama, were frequent as I was growing up, but few of these trips involved traveling on Highway 98. It wasn't until my college days that my involvement with that highway became more common. It was on one of those trips with my brother Randy that I commented on a church under construction. It had a foundation and a partial frame in place. The problem was this initial phase of building had stopped two years earlier. The work had ended. This shell had become a monument to an unfinished work. Its foundation, no matter how well laid, had not been of any value.

To build a growing church, the body of Christ must move beyond the foundation to erecting the structure. This framework is represented in the Great Commission in two parts, baptism and teaching. After Christ tells us to go into all the world preaching the gospel, he says to baptize them. "Baptism symbolizes what God has done for us in redemption."[1] It is the step of obedience following the "coming to a saving knowledge of Christ"; not that baptism saves. It finds its place on the backside of redemption as a result of evangelism.

Evangelism is the privilege we have of sharing Christ with a collapsing lost world. It is leading people to Christ. Rick Warren says that "evangelism is more than our responsibility; it is our great privilege. We are invited to be a part of bringing people into God's eternal family."[2]

This task becomes much easier when we are trained. Our churches are negligent in this area. "42 percent of Southern Baptist and 20 percent of United Methodist churches surveyed said they offered evangelism training — 22 percent of Southern Baptist and 20 percent United Methodist were from growing churches."[3]

The period of time in my ministry in central Mississippi, after having been trained in The Roman Road and CWT (Continuing Witnessing Training), was the most rewarding. Seeing the 36 decisions and then being asked to baptize those made public was a spiritual mountaintop. With my pastor standing by my side, I with great joy said, "I baptize you, my little brother or sister, in the name of God the Father, Son, and Holy Spirit. Buried with Christ, raised in newness of life." God had honored my training.

Then the challenge began for me to move each new convert toward maturity. I soon learned most of the "decisions" were genuine; the new Christians only needed nurturing.

Conversion and subsequent baptism must be framed with care so as to produce authentic, spirit-directed decisions for Christ. In construction, as a general rule, the greater the roof span, the more complicated the structure supporting the roof becomes and the narrower the range of suitable materials. If the roof represents our discipling and the materials are our new converts, then the greater God demands in discipleship, the more intense the structure (baptism and teaching) supporting the discipling becomes and the narrower the range of new converts. In other words, our evangelism and baptism must produce Christians that follow Christ even when he places great demands on them. In Jesus' day, great crowds followed as long as he did miracles. Fewer ventured to keep his admonition to "take up your cross and follow me."

When I asked pastors, "Does your church take great care in making sure new converts understand the demands of discipleship?"

sixty percent of Southern Baptist said yes; 60 percent of United Methodist; and 77 percent of Presbyterian USA said yes.[4] This was encouraging to hear. Yet, why are so many falling by the wayside? Consider this.

The 36 new Christians became my kids. Mine, in the sense I kept them in my heart and mind to be prayed for daily. It was impossible though to meet their spiritual needs alone. I had to have help. My youth leaders and other spiritual adults came to my rescue. We assigned them little brothers and sisters, and we were able to nurture growth. Did we grow all of them? No. 85 percent of those baptized moved on in their walk with the Lord. The other 15 percent fell by the wayside. Our attention to ongoing growth was pivotal in the production of the positive side of these statistics.

Evangelism and ensuing baptism must also be framed with caution because it identifies the new convert with Christ and his church. Rick Warren, in answering why baptism was so important to be included in the Great Commission said, "Because it symbolizes one of the purposes of the church — fellowship — identification with the body of Christ."[5]

In construction, structural materials have a particular weight to strength ratio, cost, and durability. The weight of discipleship on the strength of a genuine baptism is one that will endure to the end.

The survival rate of the 36 new Christians rested on how well our leadership provided individual attention to the growth process and to seeing that baptism followed soon after decision. Each new teen convert was assigned one mature adult and one mature teenager who would then pray for, spend time with them, and be there to pick them up if they fell. The close attention to discipling and the genuine faith of these mentors were pivotal in keeping these teens maturing.

Unfortunately, the churches in my 3/3/50 survey paint a far different picture. I asked, "Does your church have any kind of teaming or big brother system where you put a new Christian with a mature Christian so they can be discipled and nurtured?" Only 9 percent said yes; 91 percent said no among Southern Baptist; 89 percent of Presbyterian USA said no; as did 80 percent United Methodist.[6]

Maturing comes from identification with the body of Christ through baptism, followed by intentional nourishing. The cost of baptism is everything — one dies to self and lives for Christ — with the help of the body. The durability of this baptism is eternal: forever verifying the baptized belong to Christ and his church.

To help you know if your church has erected the structure of baptism, use the following questionnaire as a tool.

Baptism Questionnaire

	never	some	often	always
1. Our church has ongoing evangelism.	1	2	3	4
2. Our church offers evangelism training.	1	2	3	4
3. Our staff are soul winners.	1	2	3	4
4. Our ministries are evangelistic in nature.	1	2	3	4
5. Our evangelism is relational.	1	2	3	4
6. Great care is taken to make sure our new converts' decisions and baptism are genuine.	1	2	3	4

7. Great care is taken to make sure our new converts understand that baptism identifies them with the body of Christ.	never	some	often	always
	1	2	3	4

8. Great care is taken to make sure our new converts understand the demands of discipleship.	never	some	often	always
	1	2	3	4

9. Our worship has an emphasis on evangelism.	never	some	often	always
	1	2	3	4

10. The contractors (congregation) understand that the owner (God) expects the architects (pastor and staff, bishop, or elder board) to lead the church in fulfilling the Great Commission.	never	some	often	always
	1	2	3	4

Use the following to tabulate your score:
   1-10 = Poor structure
   11-20 = Fair structure; needs shoring up!
   21-30 = Good structure; build on it!
   32-40 = Excellent structure; maintain the quality!

The second structural material used in an effective house plan for church growth is that of teaching. "Teach means to bring those who are redeemed and baptized into a deeper relationship with Christ and into a better understanding of His will."[7]

Such teaching should always be Christ-centered. The study of God's Word should always point toward Christ. One of the dangers of the many resource materials we have available is that of studying the resources and not the Scriptures. Devotional books, inspirational readings, and study helps have their place, but they should not replace the Bible as our textbook. When they do, Christ ultimately will not be the central focus of our teaching.

Such was the case of a Methodist church in the Bible Belt. A few of our adults visited this church on a Sunday morning, only to find out that Bibles in the hands of church members were an unwelcome sight. The teenagers of these visiting families were even made fun of for having brought them. It is no wonder that the teaching of this church was found to be directly linked to the New Age Movement. The only way to keep our teaching Christ-centered is to give God's Word its rightful place — at the heart of all we do.

Our teaching should always be aimed at members' needs. If needs are met on a weekly basis, then the back door (members leaving) of our churches will close, effectively stopping the drain of resources. Thom S. Rainer in his book, *The Book Of Church Growth*, asks the questions, "Is it possible then that the role of Sunday school may be shifting to retention more than outreach? Or to use church growth vernacular, will Sunday school become a method of closing the 'back door' instead of opening the front door?"[8]

Most outreach these days is being promoted through the Sunday school. Rightly so. I contend, as addressed in chapters 1 and 2, that you cannot join evangelism and outreach with a fixed program unless the program becomes evangelism. In addition, no other ministry area is better equipped to meet needs and retain people than in the small group of a Sunday school class.

Bill, one Sunday morning, walked the aisle and received Christ as his Lord and Savior. Having recently moved to town, Bill and his wife Callie were seeking a place to belong. With a new-found faith, a recent marriage (they had been married six months), and a new business venture, the potential for back door loss was high. Our church slammed the door shut by immediately getting them into a young-married's Sunday school class that had the reputation for being loving and caring. Through the Christ-centered teaching of a skilled teacher the couple was nurtured.

Security was provided for Bill and Callie as the church chose to frequent the new business and provide counsel on marriage dangers from a mature married couple. This training and the disciplines of prayer, Bible reading, and worship attendance provided Bill and Callie a handle for continued growth in our church. They continue to feel that they belong with us. Waylon Moore says, "New believers have the need for love, nourishment, protection, and training."[9] When all four of these needs are present, we will retain new members.

As in the shaping of a building, the structural material of teaching will also have its weight-to-strength ratio, cost, and durability. The weight of discipleship will only be as strong as the depth of Christ-centered teaching. A tremendous amount of time, energy, and prayer will be the cost of teaching to meet needs. The durability of your teaching will be measured by how well the truth of God's Word is rightly divided.

Accuracy in the fundamental truths of God's Word will erect a growth frame that is flawless in its message. You should be open to questions of faith but steer seekers to the unique qualities of our beliefs that make us Christian. "An unreliable messenger can cause a lot of trouble; reliable communication permits progress" (Proverbs 13:17 NIV). The ageless truths of God's Word being taught provide reliable communication ... communication that is correctly discerned. "Highly effective churches are very selective about whom they endorse as teachers."[10] A nightmare for any minister is to have a teacher who is oblivious to members' needs, who teaches heresy, and whose instruction is not Christ-centered. If such is the case, growth will not occur.

We have also had teachers who had Christ at the center, members' needs at the forefront, and taught the truths of God's Word but destroyed class growth. Why? They were boring teachers. Dr. Bruce Wilkerson in *Teaching With Style* says, "The #1 worldwide hindrance to learning is boredom."[11]

Boredom will be replaced with excitement when there is excellence in presentation. "Only the most deeply committed adults (or most foolish) will keep attending a Bible class taught by an incompetent teacher."[12]

At our central Mississippi church, our youth Sunday school enrollment went from 60 to 90 — to moving toward 120 in three years. Attendance followed the same incremental increases. The reason for this growth resides in the fact that we insisted on excellence. Our classes were not boring. They were the essence of life.

George Barna tells us, "In today's society, commitment to satisfying felt needs through excellence in effort is the only sure ticket to growth."[13] I would substitute "real" for "felt" and Barna would be right on target.

Rick Warren adds that "if you study healthy churches, you'll discover that when God finds a church that is doing a quality job of winning, nurturing, equipping, and sending out believers, he sends that church plenty of raw material. On the other hand, why would God send a lot of prospects to a church that doesn't know what to do with them? Quality attracts quality."[14]

"Research shows," according to Rick Warren, "that people today are seeking institutions which provide high quality output. Churches are no different. Those congregations which expect, create, and celebrate excellence in their activities have the potential for expansion."[15]

Have you ever had your expectations for something on a certain level only to find the ultimate product was far superior to what you thought it would be? Such was the case of a media library. My head swelled with pride every time I walked by it, and I had nothing to do with it. Its quality drew people in to read its books. Our teaching should have the same standard of excellence. We should be as Paul when he said, "By the grace God has given me, I laid the foundation as an expert builder" (1 Corinthians 3:10). Our structure of teaching should be put in place as a skillful craftsman — one that says it's the best our church has to offer.

In our 3/3/50 Church Growth Survey, Southern Baptist response to "How would you describe the teaching in your church?" was, 20 percent said excellent, 66 percent good, 11 percent fair, and 3 percent no response. United Methodist described theirs as 40 percent excellent, 40 percent good, and 20 percent fair. Presbyterians responded with 77 percent good; 11 percent fair; with 12 percent no response. If your church falls into the good rating, it's your chal-

lenge to move it to the excellent column. It's a worthy challenge —
a reachable goal.

To help you know if your church has erected the structure of
teaching, use the following evaluation.

Teaching Evaluation

	never	some	often	always
1. All of our teaching is Christ-centered.				
	1	2	3	4
2. The Bible is our teacher's textbook.	never	some	often	always
	1	2	3	4
3. Our teaching is deliberately aimed at "real" needs.	never	some	often	always
	1	2	3	4
4. Our teachers rightly divide the Word of God.	never	some	often	always
	1	2	3	4
5. Our teaching is done with excellence.	never	some	often	always
	1	2	3	4

Use the following to tabulate your score:

5-10 = Poor teaching; begin tearing down old structure.

11-15 = Good teaching; needs work in certain areas.

16-20 = Excellent teaching; maintain but shore up areas that
rob you of a perfect score.

Make a note of your score. We will return later to address the
weaknesses in your church teaching.

My in-laws live in a double-wide trailer on a twenty-acre pecan orchard. You would think the anchors that come with the trailer would be sufficient to affix it to the ground in case of a storm. My father-in-law thinks differently. So he fastened everything to the ground with additional moorings — from straps over the top to attachments to his ranch style porch. No strong wind was going to destroy his trailer without a fight.

Our church growth structures of baptism and teaching, even done with excellence, may not be sufficient to moor our people, to ground them in their faith. We must anchor the frame to provide stability when the storms of life come.

---

1. Mims, *Kingdom Principles For Church Growth*, p. 28.

2. Warren, *The Purpose Driven Church*, p. 104.

3. 3/3/50 Church Growth Survey by author. Note: Presbyterian USA church registered no evangelism training. This has a lot to do with their predestination view of salvation and emphasis on infant baptism.

4. *Ibid.*

5. Warren, *The Purpose Driven Church*, p. 84.

6. 3/3/50 Church Growth Survey by author.

7. Mims, *Kingdom Principles For Church Growth*, p. 29.

8. Rainer, *The Book Of Church Growth*, p. 292.

9. Waylon Moore, *New Testament Follow-up* (Grand Rapids, Michigan: William B. Eerdmans Company, 1963), pp. 24-26.

10. Barna, *The Habits Of Highly Effective Churches*, p. 137.

11. Dr. Bruce Wilkerson, *Teaching With Style (Video Series)* (Nashville, Tennessee: Convention Press, 1995), p. vii.

12. John R. Cionca, *Solving Church Education's Ten Toughest Problems* (Wheaton, Illinois: Victor Books, 1990), p. 103.

13. Barna, *User Friendly Churches*, p. 112.

14. Warren, *The Purpose Driven Church*, p. 51.

15. George Barna, *Successful Churches: What They Have In Common* (Ventura, California: Regal Books, 1990), p. 27.

Chapter Six

The Anchoring Of The Frame

A story is told by Robert Byrne in a book written in 1984 of a skyscraper in New York City that was blown over by a high wind. Built on the old Madison Square Garden site, this building towered 700 feet high. Because of underhanded dealings, it included substandard concrete. A rare New York storm brought lateral pressure on the building, overcoming the resistance of the foundation and toppling the structure over. Byrne's book is fiction, a novel with a strangely prophetic ring to it. It captures all our fears, or at least our curiosity, about the stability of skyscrapers. Many of us have experienced the feeling of the top floors moving a foot or two back and forth when visiting a high building. Our fears are eased when we realize the sheer weight of all the components — concrete, steel, masonry — is enough to keep it in position, provided the weight is supported by the foundations.

The sheer weight of discipleship brings stability to our church body construction. And at no time has this stability been more needed than now. "In recent studies, we discovered that a majority of people who made a decision for Christ were no longer connected to a Christian church. Within a short period — usually eight to twelve weeks — after their initial decision."[1] The structures of baptism and teaching provide the framework for discipleship and this connection to continue, thereby enabling disciples to be supported and nurtured.

In the construction business, lateral stability is provided by diagonal braces or anchors. Stability provided by discipleship is moored when there is a sense of fellowship among believers, accountability to one another, and periodic spiritual growth evaluation.

New Christians gain strength when they are drawn into experiencing fellowship in Christ's body. "The Christian life is not just a matter of believing," says Rick Warren, "it includes belonging. Once people have made a commitment to Christ, they need to be encouraged to take the next step and commit to Christ's body, the local church."[2]

As a new Christian joins hands with other believers in fellowship, the strength of one is shared with the stability of many. The live loads of change, tragedy, and unexpected life surprises will not cause us to give under the stresses of life because the frame has been strengthened from one to many through fellowship.

Janie was a mother of two whose husband worked in the construction industry. Having recently accepted Christ, her faith was tested when her husband fell from a scaffold and was killed. Fortunately, Janie had been drawn into the fellowship along with her husband through a couples' Sunday school class prior to the accident. Immediately upon hearing the news, several of the young women were at her side. Through the funeral and the grief process, class members continued to show compassion and ministered to Janie and her children. A year and a half later, God brought a new person into her life. The spiritual journey she entered prior to the accident has become stronger as she continues to grow along with her class.

A church will be built up in maturity, experience authentic discipleship and growth, as long as fellowship is present. Otherwise growth will be limited. Darrell Robinson in his book *Total Church Life* says, "A church will never grow beyond its fellowship. If the fellowship is right, the church will continue to minister, witness in love, and be built up in maturity and in number. But if the fellowship is not right the church will decline and eventually die."[3]

The pages of church history can be filled with the tragedy of splintered, bruised, and broken fellowships. Trace the cause of most declining churches and you will find church families torn asunder by unresolved conflict and poor fellowship. Corinthians 1:10 (LB) says, "Let there be real harmony so that there won't be splits in the church ... Be of one mind, united in thought and purpose."

"The key to harmony is to be united in purpose."[4] Discipleship will be nurtured if we rally around a common purpose that fosters good fellowship.

When fellowship and unity take hold of a church — watch out, God is getting ready to do a mighty work. Such was the case with a youth group of mine. It got to the point where our love was so deep, nothing could stop the flow of youth coming our way. I would walk into choir rehearsal and I could hear a pin drop. They hung on to every word I said. Rehearsals were interrupted weekly with teenagers raising their hands and saying, "Brother Danny, I wanted to let you know, Johnny accepted Christ as his Lord and Savior today." When I resigned, teenagers were testifying all over the church, and I couldn't tell you who they were. The group had grown so fast. Why? Because genuine fellowship had taken root.

A byproduct of having God's people in loving, close relationships with each other through fellowship is that the resources are in place to provide for accountability. "Accountability is not a closed-ended, once-a-year process that can be completed in a two-week period of energetic self-examination. Highly effective churches constantly reflect on their status and progress and perpetually strive to improve."[5] And they do it in close relationship with each other.

This diagonal brace or anchor in our construction is necessary to provide the encouragement to live out the demands of discipleship. Only close relationships will work in an accountability partnership because each partner must be able to love as well as confront, encourage as well as reprimand.

This accountability must first begin with a set of guidelines. These guidelines must govern what we do as a church, what we do in relationship to each other. We must be able to enforce them.

David Hocking in his book *The Seven Laws of Christian Leadership* says, "If you cannot enforce your guidelines, you might have the wrong set of guidelines or you yourself may be lacking in good leadership."[6]

Once guidelines are in place, then each youth and adult within the framework of close relationships needs to have a discipleship accountability partner. These partners covet to love, pray, guide, confront, and nurture each other. As much as possible, a younger Christian needs to be placed with a more mature Christian.

We did this through our "Care Volunteer Ministry." Though it initially created a lot of unnecessary paper work, once we streamlined it, the ministry did the job of providing an accountability discipleship partnership. Spiritual maturity was the end result.

A natural chain of accountability exists with staff to pastor, church musicians to music minister, teachers to minister of education, etc. Or, in the case of many church bodies, the pastor is accountable to the elder board, elder board to the regional body, and regional body to a national body. Each church leader should be accountable to someone as well as have others who are responsible to him or her. Each should have the freedom to love, confront, affirm, and rebuke in love. With that may come the need for change if an individual fails to carry out his or her known responsibilities.

Restoration must be attempted if this action is taken. A new place of service and accountability should then be provided once restored.

We are in dire need of addressing this area in our churches. In our 3/3/50 Church Growth Survey, when asked, "Does your church have any system of accountability built into it related to attendance, outreach, discipline, or discipleship?" 83 percent of Southern Baptists, 45 percent of Presbyterians, and 100 percent of United Methodists said no.[7] "Accountability is one of the differentiating points between churches that maintain great leadership and those that experience erratic quality and high turnover of leadership."[8]

The longer a church has been in existence, the harder it is to provide accountability. I have found in First churches that prayer works wonders in changing people who are power controllers or who lack spiritual vitality — either by removing them or bringing

70

about a spiritual transformation. Until they regained spiritual vitality, we ascertained their gifts and plugged them into something of interest, away from spiritual decision making.

Accountability and restoration used to be an accepted practice in our churches. In recent years, the First Baptist Church of Macon, Mississippi, ran across some of its old records. In a report of a business meeting during the Civil War, the story is told of a Confederate soldier who was disbarred from the fellowship because of an unnamed sin. They had received a letter from him after he had left to fight asking for forgiveness and to be restored to fellowship with the church. The church lovingly voted to forgive and restore the young man.

It would be to our good if we would again institute the practice of accountability, both of sin and of known responsibility, and of the lost doctrine of restoration.

The final brace in providing for discipleship is that of having periodic spiritual growth evaluation. This is done on an individual level through personal accountability. On a church-wide level, the church leadership should get together once a quarter and determine where the church is in its spiritual growth. Sunday school classes can evaluate using a Sunday school hour at the end of a quarter; discipleship classes can evaluate the same way. Once reports have been collected, an extended staff meeting can be used to examine reports and make necessary changes so as to achieve the desired growth in discipleship. The following questionnaire can be used for classes to make their reports.

Spiritual Growth Evaluation

Class Name _____

On the basis of where you believe your class is spiritually, please circle the appropriate number with 1 being the least amount of understanding and 10 complete understanding;

1. Conversion Evangelism
   *God cares for you
       1 2 3 4 5 6 7 8 9 10

   *The person of Jesus Christ
       1 2 3 4 5 6 7 8 9 10

   *The work of Christ
       1 2 3 4 5 6 7 8 9 10

   *The Spirit within you
       1 2 3 4 5 6 7 8 9 10

2. Comprehension Evangelism
   *The obedient Christian
       1 2 3 4 5 6 7 8 9 10

   *God's Word in your life
       1 2 3 4 5 6 7 8 9 10

   *Conversing with God
       1 2 3 4 5 6 7 8 9 10

   *Fellowship with Christians
       1 2 3 4 5 6 7 8 9 10

   *Witnessing for Christ
       1 2 3 4 5 6 7 8 9 10

3. Confirmation Evangelism
   *Maturing in Christ
   1   2   3   4   5   6   7   8   9   10

   *The Lordship of Christ
   1   2   3   4   5   6   7   8   9   10

   *Faith and the promises of God
   1   2   3   4   5   6   7   8   9   10

   *Knowing God's will
   1   2   3   4   5   6   7   8   9   10

   *Walking as a servant
   1   2   3   4   5   6   7   8   9   10

   *The call to fruitful living
   1   2   3   4   5   6   7   8   9   10

   *Genuine love in action
   1   2   3   4   5   6   7   8   9   10

   *Purity of life
   1   2   3   4   5   6   7   8   9   10

   *Integrity in living
   1   2   3   4   5   6   7   8   9   10

   *Character in action
   1   2   3   4   5   6   7   8   9   10

   *Who is God?
   1   2   3   4   5   6   7   8   9   10

   *The authority of God's Word
   1   2   3   4   5   6   7   8   9   10

*The Holy Spirit

   1 2 3 4 5 6 7 8 9 10

*Spiritual warfare

   1 2 3 4 5 6 7 8 9 10

*The return of Christ

   1 2 3 4 5 6 7 8 9 10

4. Community Awareness Evangelism

*What is a disciple?

   1 2 3 4 5 6 7 8 9 10

*The responsible steward

   1 2 3 4 5 6 7 8 9 10

*Helping others find Christ

   1 2 3 4 5 6 7 8 9 10

*Follow-up

   1 2 3 4 5 6 7 8 9 10

*World vision[9]

   1 2 3 4 5 6 7 8 9 10

Each class member should fill out one of these based on his/ her understanding. After individual members fill them out, they should be collected and the numbers added for each and then divided by the number who filled out an evaluation. This will give you an average for that class. Transfer this information to a blank form and turn it in to the church office with class records.

As a staff, use the following scoring to determine the results. Our spiritual understanding is:

    0- 50 = poor
    51-100 = fair
    101-150 = good
    151-200 = excellent

In order for you to see where your church stands in developing the covering of discipleship based on this chapter, use the following as a tool.

1. Our church fellowship is	poor	fair	good	excellent
	1	2	3	4
2. Our fellowship is close in the good times and bad.	poor	fair	good	excellent
	1	2	3	4
3. The understanding of our purpose as a church is	poor	fair	good	excellent
	1	2	3	4
4. Our system of accountability is	poor	fair	good	excellent
	1	2	3	4
5. The job we do of evaluating spiritual growth is	poor	fair	good	excellent
	1	2	3	4
6. According to the spiritual growth results from the survey above, our spiritual understanding is	poor	fair	good	excellent
	1	2	3	4

Use the following scoring to see how your church is doing in framing the cover of discipleship:

    1- 6 = poorly; begin laying some braces.
    7-12 = fair; add some stability with a few more anchors.
    13-18 = good; firmly plant those braces you have in place.
    19-24 = excellent; disciples are being grown!

Using the results of building the house, erecting the structure, and anchoring the frame, let's begin to frame the work as we seek to reach people and build a thriving, growing church for Christ's kingdom.

---

1. Barna, *The Habits Of Highly Effective Churches*, p. 121.

2. Warren, *The Purpose Driven Church*, p. 132.

3. Darrell W. Robinson, *Total Church Life* (Nashville, Tennessee: Broadman Press, 1990), p. 34.

4. Warren, *The Purpose Driven Church*, p. 86.

5. Barna, *The Habits Of Highly Effective Churches*, p. 70.

6. David Hocking, *The Seven Laws Of Christian Leadership* (Ventura, California: Regal Books, 1991), pp. 258-259.

7. 3/3/50 Church Growth Survey by author.

8. Barna, *The Habits Of Highly Effective Churches*, p. 52.

9. *Design For Discipleship* (Colorado Springs, Colorado: Nav Press, 1994). Note: These are the subtitles from the six books in *Design For Discipleship*.

Chapter Seven

Framing The Work

My father-in-law is a designer, of sorts. If you give him time, he will figure out a better way of doing something. His ten-acre pecan orchard now houses his shop where he frames — designs his improvements — so a task can be done more easily, better, and with greater output.

He does it by altering the original structure, eliminating unnecessary parts, or by adding a piece to speed the process. Whether it is a pole welded to his tractor to shake his pecan trees or a redesigned haybailer, Doc finds a way to improve the structural design so that it is a much enhanced product.

So can it be with churches. The basic frame may be present for growth to occur, yet it goes lacking. The original structure may need altering ... an unnecessary ministry or staff position eliminated ... a new outreach program or personnel added. Knowing what structure is effective and what isn't is the first step in altering the ministry for growth.

Non-Effective Ways To Structure For Growth

Most non-growing churches structure to reach people by over-structuring, under- or non-structuring, or structuring programmatically but not evangelically.

Over-structuring is done in either one or two ways. Churches will hire more professional staff than their membership warrants or attempt to program for more ministries than they have people available to staff them. The result, a lot going on with little results. Among growing churches, our 3/3/50 survey revealed 9 percent of Southern Baptist and 22 percent of United Methodist pastors classified their churches as over-structured.[1]

In a nearby city, you can walk through the doors of First Baptist Church and see a long hallway with nothing but staff offices. When a church is over-staffed, generally that is a sign the church hired staff to do the work of the laity.

In *How To Grow A Church*, Don McGavran quotes Neil Braum by saying, "He studied the churches around the world in terms of the proportion of paid staff to the membership of the church and found that usually when the number of paid staff is high, a non-growing church results."[2] A general rule of thumb is one staff member for every 200 members in attendance. At that point leadership must be given away if growth is to continue.

Plateaued or declining churches hinder their ascent from level growth or decline by trying to maintain the same structure they had when they were larger. When positions of leadership exceed available people willing to fill them, several things happen. Quality suffers. You will have positions not filled or positions filled with people who don't really want to serve. Burnout will result. A constant turnover in leadership becomes the norm.

Millie, a vibrant mother of three, held a number of jobs in the church. She was pianist for two choirs and an ensemble, taught Sunday school, worked with mission organizations, served on the Weekday Education committee, and helped with Mother's Day Out. In addition, she taught school, had six piano students, was active in the Women's Club, and raised her children while her husband worked off-shore. It was no wonder Millie was no longer her vibrant self and began to drop out of things at church. It wasn't long before she was no longer in church at all. Burnout had set in and the church was partially to blame.

Some non-growing churches structure to reach people by under- or non-structuring. With regard to staff, they have more people than one full-time person can possibly minister to. Or they staff their Sunday school or other ministries with a skeleton crew with little help to handle the large numbers in that class or ministry.

It is surprising how many churches build Family Life Centers but fail to consider who will plan and run the programming. It takes a full-time staff member. Even more astonishing is how many churches will hire a full-time staff member but provide him/her no clerical help.

The reason we went from five music groups to thirteen in our south Mississippi church was largely due to a quality secretary. She handled the tasks I delegated and freed me to promote involvement of people through music.

With regard to adequate ministries, some churches choose not to structure. The fewer ministries the better for them. The result is a church with few opportunities for members to use their gifts, minimal ways to involve people in ministry, and a message to the community that says, "Not much is happening here." Surprisingly, of the 29 percent of all the churches who said they were under-structured in our 3/3/50 survey, 11 percent came from growing churches.[3] Presbyterian USA churches claimed the higher percentage of 44 percent under-structured.

Salem Church is an example. Salem is content to have one class for everybody on Sunday. They have one service on Sundays — Sunday morning. They do not keep records. Its members come. Its members go. That's it. Is it a growing church? I think not!

The number one characteristic of most non-growing churches is that they do have a structure in place but it is programmatic and not evangelical. Of the 31 percent of SBC churches who said they were structured wrong, a whopping 17 percent came from growing churches.[4] Twenty percent and 22 percent of United Methodist and Presbyterian USA churches, respectively, characterized themselves this way.

George Barna in *User Friendly Churches* says, "Jesus did not minister through programs. The early church did not appoint program managers. The Bible never exhorts us to create new programs. Jesus, the apostles, the Bible — all indicate by word or deed that our focus is to be on people, through meaningful relationships."[5] The greater the embracing of the Great Commission through relationships, the greater the growth.

"Without the driving force of the Great Commission," says Gene Mims, "church growth will be little more than a misguided attempt to gain numbers, discover methods, and do something different."[6] Declining or plateaued churches have lost sight of the Great Commission. They are busy with many activities and programs, but these are an end in themselves. Instead of offering an aerobics class for the purpose of locating people who are without Christ and following up on the prospects found, they offer aerobics for the sake of aerobics. It may be a service but it's not a ministry. Instead of offering a Mother's Day Out as a way of locating young families with children as prospects for evangelism and church membership, these churches are thinking of themselves, providing a service for its constituents with little thought for outreach.

You have been there. The call goes out one Sunday morning for men to play in the church basketball league. That's great — until you hear the next statement: "But you must be a member of our church to play." If you are serious about fulfilling the Great Commission, that statement cuts to the heart.

> *Two pastors, Wylie Fredricks and Jim King, were ministers at sister churches in the sprawling suburbs of a large city. The churches, of similar size and composition, were within ten miles of each other. Both were surrounded by literally thousands of lost and unchurched persons.*
>
> *Fredricks and King, who had been friends in seminary, came to be pastors of the churches about the same time. Realizing they must build bridges to their communities, both were very much oriented toward ministry. (Bridge building is the Community Awareness Evangelism frame to be introduced later in this chapter.)*

Fredricks, at Sisterville Church, began a day-care center, a program for the elderly, and literacy classes for the people who lived in his community. The program, along with recreation ministries and work with poverty-level people, soon reached 700 persons a week.

King, at Calvary Church, also began work in day-care ministries. He established work with the deaf, alcoholics, poverty-level people, senior citizens, young people, illiterates, and prisoners. Soon, he was working with some 800 people a week.

King led Calvary to explosive growth. Every Sunday morning people were saved. Each week many people were baptized. The church, which had been averaging 100 persons in attendance, zoomed to more than 1,000.

Fredricks operated the same sort of outreach programs yet remained at 100 in attendance. The ministry program overbalanced the church budget. The hard-pressed members rebelled. They asked Fredricks to leave.

Calvary grew because the ministries reached into the community, building bridges. The ministries were a springboard to witness, and witness to professions of faith. The ministries were part of the church, expanding into evangelism and outreach.

Sisterville failed because Fredricks forgot why he was building bridges. He would not use the ministries for evangelistic purposes. "We would be manipulating people if we witnessed to them after we got them in for the programs," he said. Nothing, therefore, was said about Christ or redemption at Sisterville Church.

One grew and one failed because one maintained a redemptive note, and the other forgot why it was out on the bridge.[7]

We must begin to ask the right questions of our church people. How is our church structured? How can we provide the framework by God's design to reach people? Facing up to these questions will bring a new understanding of how the church does its work.

An Effective Way To Structure Growth

An effective way churches structure to reach and assimilate people is to frame the work. Framing the work means to focus or structure the work of the church, providing a framework by God's design to accomplish the task of reaching and assimilation. Much like a builder takes a blueprint of a home, frames it, and builds a beautiful dwelling, we take God's blueprint, frame the work he has for us, and then build a beautiful dwelling by his Spirit for the expanding and growing body of Christ. This framework, in the New Testament design, uses programs to enhance evangelism, not to replace it. It is structured so that a new program can bring life when it replaces an old, unproductive program. It will flourish because it takes evangelism out of fixed traditions.

The structures we build are for the purpose of ministry. In the book *Successful Churches: What They Have In Common*, Barna Research tells us that in successful churches, "Structure was viewed as a support system, a means to an end, rather than an end in itself. The structures they used had been developed, accepted, implemented, re-evaluated, and upgraded. At all times, the focus was upon ministry, not structure."[8] The following planks are designed with that understanding in mind. I give them in brief here, followed by an in-depth look in coming chapters.

* Plank One

Community Awareness Evangelism is the *going* of the Great Commission. The days are over when people will come to our churches just by seeing our buildings on the corner. People, as observers, want to know we care. We do so by being creative with the kinds of activities we offer to meet real needs of people. Our strategy of outreach will be to *g*enerate a needs list in the community, *o*rganize the project to meet the need, *i*nitiate the project, *n*ail down follow-up plans, and *g*ravitate those at the end of the follow-up back to a new beginning of the same project.

* Plank Two

Conversion Evangelism is the *baptizing them* of the Great Commission. It is the conscious effort of seeking to win to Christ those we have identified in the community awareness plank of our frame. Through the gospel presentation we allow the Holy Spirit to make followers of Christ. Our strategy will be to go to the "lost sheep" (Matthew 10:6), preach or declare the "gospel" (Matthew 10:7), minister "freely" (Matthew 10:8), and be "wise and harmless" (Matthew 10:16).

* Plank Three

Comprehension Evangelism is the *teaching all nations* of the Great Commission. It is the concerted effort to place siding to the frame by moving the new convert into the fellowship of a small group, thereby becoming a learner. Our strategy will be to team them with a mature Christian, enlist them in a new members class, access an "in touch" plan, capture the class spirit for the new convert (both discussed later), and help them progress pass spiritual infancy. (How? You'll see.)

* Plank Four

Confirmation Evangelism is the *making disciples* of the Great Commission. It is the progression from spiritual infancy to spiritual maturity. Our strategy will be to develop spiritual growth prerequisites in the areas of Bible study, prayer, worship, fellowship, and the sharing of one's faith. This completed structure will lead people to be doers, reproducing followers and leading others to maturity in Christ.

The overpass in Houston, mentioned in chapter 1, cost the state of Texas a million dollars but it was easily fixed by adding a section to the existing structure. The platform that collapsed, referred to in chapter 2, was quickly removed and another was soon in its place. My father-in-law's quick eye for improvements made haste of any substandard tool. But the structuring of our churches is not easily fixed when they have been framed wrong, nor can they be quickly removed and another put in its place. But the understanding of how to frame the work will move you a step closer to taking down an old frame one plank at a time and to begin building a magnificent structure for God's glory. Let's take a closer look at each of these new planks and begin to frame the work.

1. 3/3/50 Church Growth Survey by author.

2. Donald McGavran and Win Arn, *How To Grow A Church* (Ventura, California: Regal Books, 1982), p. 114 (tenth printing).

3. 3/3/50 Church Growth Survey by author.

4. *Ibid.*

5. Barna, *User Friendly Churches*, pp. 42-43.

6. Mims, *Kingdom Principles For Church Growth*, p. 20.

7. Jack Reford, *Planting New Churches* (Nashville, Tennessee: Broadman Press, 1978), pp. 12-13.

8. *Successful Churches: What They Have In Common*, Barna Research Group, Glendale, California, 1990, p. 33.

Chapter Eight

Framing With Community Awareness Evangelism

How aware is your community of your church? I asked this of the fifty churches in our 3/3/50 survey and among Southern Baptist, 17 percent were little aware, 63 percent some, 11 percent a lot, and 6 percent not aware; Presbyterians scored 33 percent a little aware, 55 percent some, and 11 percent not aware; Methodist came in at 60 percent little aware and 40 percent some aware. It goes without saying — the level of community awareness needs raising.

Our south Mississippi church at one time was one of only two churches in town; the other was the United Methodist Church. Both to this day sit back-to-back in the middle of town. But now there is a difference! Thirty years have passed and the area now sports eleven Southern Baptist churches with 64 other churches of various denominations scattered throughout the county. The community is not as aware of the presence of the original two churches as it once was.

With the availability of many more options for church involvement and secular distractions, the general public is being more selective of where it spends its time and commitment. Denominational loyalty is no longer a driving force determining where a person attends church. A recent survey by Barna Research found "denominational affiliation to be of only moderate importance — and that was found predominately among Catholic parishioners."[1]

As people observe our church, they are wanting to know if those who are meeting behind its enclosed walls really care about each other. 53 percent of church go-ers say caring for each other is extremely important in choosing a church.[2] Are we really interested in real needs? The church that best answers this question in demonstrable ways will reap the harvest.

In answering why people come back to our churches the second time, Lyle Schaller in his research says "that the younger visitors emphasize how the first experience spoke to their religious needs."[3]

Where do we start then to meet the real religious needs of people? "The community is your starting point," says Rick Warren. "It is the pool of lost people who live within driving distance of your church that have made no commitment at all to either Jesus Christ or your church. They are the unchurched that you want to reach. Your community is where the purpose of evangelism takes place. This community awareness evangelism can take place when we are creative in the kinds of activities that reveal prospects for evangelism."

In developing a strategy for implementing this plank, we will need to generate a needs list of our community, organize the project to meet the need, initiate the project, nail down follow-up plans, and gravitate those at the end of the follow-up back to a new beginning of the same project. This strategy becomes the *going* of fulfilling the Great Commission.

* G — Generate A Need List

Common sense tells us that in order to meet needs we first must know what those needs are. A first step would be to do a church and community profile of a ten-mile area around your church. This would include a ten-year growth analysis of your

86

church and a demographic portrait of your city. For Southern Baptist churches this can be obtained from the Leavell Center For Evangelism and Church Growth at the New Orleans Baptist Theological Seminary or LifeWay Christian Resources in Nashville. Other denominations can get the demographics from the U.S. Census Bureau or denominational headquarters.

If requested, you should be able to secure from denominational leadership the implications for church growth based on this information. For instance, one such First Baptist church we served had the following implications for growth:

- Target Median Adults (45-64),
- Target Boomers,
- Consider A Divorce Recovery Workshop,
- Develop Ministry To Non-traditional Families, and
- Develop Seniors Ministry.

Demographics usually do not give a complete picture of the ministry needs of your community. Use the demographic data to help you develop a questionnaire to be used by your church family. For example, using the above church growth implications one could develop the following questionnaire.

Church Growth Questionnaire

Our demographics for our church have revealed some needs in the following areas. Please help us clarify these by praying about them and then giving us your input.

Name _____ (Optional)

1. What activities, events, ministries, and programs would help us reach the faithless, non-churched median age adults (45-64)?

2. What activities, events, ministries, and programs would help us reach the faithless non-churched Boomers?

3. What kind of program can we implement to address divorce in our community?

4. What ministry or ministries can we develop to reach the faithless non-traditional families?

5. What activities, events, ministries, and programs can we provide to enhance our seniors' ministry and help us reach our faithless, non-churched senior adults?

For us in central Mississippi, it was asking the question, "What can we do to reach the faithless teenagers of our community?" The answer came in the form of offering four activities: (1) Judgment House, (2) Youth Camp, (3) WOW (Win Our World) Weekend, and (4) People Need The Lord Musical. Thirty-six professions of faith was the result.

A step further in assessing the needs of your area is to do a door-to-door survey and ask three questions.

1. If you were to go to church, how would you describe the church you would most likely attend?

2. What needs do you see that you or your neighbors have that our church could plan to meet?

3. What is it about churches in general that have kept you and others from attending that our church should try to avoid?

Once all the data is obtained from the demographics, church survey, and door-to-door canvassing, it should be processed so that the staff and church leadership can meet to develop a growth frame.

* O — Organize The Projects To Meet Needs

The growth frame that is developed by the church leadership should include specific projects or ministries to meet needs. Each should have a starting date and person or persons responsible for its implementation. Saddleback Baptist Church, where Rick Warren is pastor, uses these bridge events to reach the community. They include everything from a harvest party at Halloween to a Western Day at the Fourth of July celebration. Paul Powell, in his book *How To Make A Church Hum*, majors on outreach in reaching the community by having day camps, men's rallies, ladies' luncheons, and outside services.[4]

The "Circle Of Concern," no matter the location where I've used it, has always provided media attention to focus the community on our meeting needs. It's a simple circling of the high school or city hall or whatever your focus, by candlelight and delivering a prayer of concern. Once you have the community's attention, you offer specific activities to address the concern voiced in the prayer. The results are phenomenal.

*I — Initiate The Project

The only thing worse than not planning anything is planning it and then not doing it. You can keep this from happening by developing a promotional schedule for each event and staying with it. Each project demands that you have some system for gathering basic information on each participant. This can be done through pre-registration or by some sort of sign-in procedure at the event.

If the event has never been attempted before, go overboard in your promotion. First-time happenings are always a tough sell but can go well with a saturation of publicity. Our first Discipleship Training Fair succeeded with amazing results, quadrupling our discipleship involvement because of God's timing and our media blitz during the month before.

Do not attempt to disguise an event by announcing one thing and its being something else. For instance, if you are having a divorce recovery workshop, make sure it is a divorce recovery workshop and not a veiled attempt to get names of prospects. Such a conference should be the best effort your church can make in providing help for divorcees.

N — Nail Down Follow-up Plans

Immediately following each project, follow-up needs to take place. This can be done at the last meeting where you say, "Because of the magnitude of the teenage drug problem, we in no way can address all of your concerns as parents in this one day conference. We want to give you a chance to have some input. Beginning next Monday, 6:30 p.m., we want to invite you to a six-week intensive training conference at the city library."

At the last session of that training, a gospel presentation is made. Your comments could be along the line of: "Teens need our help in dealing with drugs. Most of the time it requires more than we can give them. I, as a Christian, feel only Christ is the answer to drugs or any other problem we may face. He will help you help your teen but you must know him first. Do you mind if I share how I first met Christ and how he changed my life?"

Every community awareness evangelism follow-up needs to have the presentation of the gospel message near its conclusion. By doing so you turn a social ministry into an evangelism opportunity.

G — Gravitate Those At The End Of The Follow-up
Back To A New Beginning Of The Same Project

Those who receive Christ at the conclusion of the activity are then asked to attend a new beginning of that same project. At the first meeting, they are allowed to share what the initial conference meant to them. A live graduate who went through the course others are unsure of makes for greater potential for success in the second offering. The ultimate satisfaction comes when the new convert has been discipled to the point that he or she can now be the leader for the conference.

Look back at chapter 1 under the structure of baptism. What did your church score? Poor, fair, good, or excellent in structure? If you scored good or below, proceed with the following "frame" development.

Community Awareness Evangelism Frame Development

1. Our church can make the community more aware of its presence by having _____
   _____.

   Examples: New signs at by-pass; advertising campaign; Circle Of Concern; projects involving entire community.

2. Our church can generate a needs list by having a _____
   _____.

   Examples: Church and community profile; questionnaire by the church family; or door-to-door survey.

3. Our church can organize the following projects to meet needs by planning a _____
   _____.

   Examples: Divorce recovery workshop; literacy conference; teenagers and drugs/ teenagers and alcohol conference; Discipleship Training Fair; parenting skills conference.

4. Our church should initiate a project by _____
   _____.

   Examples: Designing a promotional schedule; developing a system for gathering information.

5. Our church can nail down follow-up plans by_____
   _____.

   Examples: Presenting gospel at the end; scheduling a more intensive and longer conference on the same subject; visit in the homes.

6. Our church can gravitate those at the end of the follow-up back to a new beginning of the same project by_____
   _____.

   Examples: Enlisting those who receive Christ to speak at the new beginning of project; pointing them out as a graduate of first conference.

1. "Americans Describe Their Ideal Church," Barna Research Group, www.barna.org, October 7, 1998.

2. "Beliefs, Caring, Sermons Draw Churchgoers," Barna Research Group, www.messenger-inquirer.com, October 24, 1998.

3. Lyle Schaller, *44 Steps Up Off The Plateau* (Nashville, Tennessee: Abingdon Press, 1993), pp. 48-49.

4. Paul Powell, *How To Make Your Church Hum* (Nashville, Tennessee: Broadman Press, 1977), pp. 66-68.

Chapter Nine

Framing With
Conversion Evangelism

Not all of those who attend each Community Awareness Evangelism project will receive Christ as personal Lord and Savior. The Conversion Evangelism plank of our structure is the conscious effort of seeking to win those who were identified in the Community Awareness Evangelism plank of our frame but did not initially respond to the gospel message. In a concerted effort, we seek to have opportunity to present the gospel message and allow the Holy Spirit to make followers of Christ. Our blueprint will take us to the "lost sheep" (Matthew 10:6), preach or declare the "gospel" (Matthew 10:7), minister "freely" (Matthew 10:8), and be wise and harmless.

Go To The Lost Sheep
Three effective ways that we can go to the lost sheep of our community is to invite them to church, love them into a relationship, and introduce them to Jesus.

* Invite Them To Church

The majority of our congregations do not share their faith on a regular basis. Only "10 percent of the church body are soul winners and have the gift of evangelism."[1] The other 80+ percent have the potential of being "inviters." It's a potential because it is presently not happening. "Regular participants in church activities," so says George Barna, "do not invite their unchurched friends and neighbors to attend with them."

One nationwide study conducted by Barna Research found that on any given Sunday morning, one out of four unchurched people would willingly attend a church service if a friend would invite them to do so. That's fifteen to twenty million adults.[2] The key is to give them tools that will remove some of the fear. A flyer, card, or special promotional item that inviters can distribute that has the basic information on the article meets this need.

The telephone is a marvelous tool. Generally, 20 percent of the number one calls to invite to church will come. Ten percent will actually join if you combine the call by a personal friend with a unique letter using the invitee's name throughout.

Recently, I picked up eight teenagers who were non-church teens. Out of 75 teens, the call and letter was all it took.

* Love Them Into A Relationship

Much can be said about the cold call evangelism of the '50s and '60s. Lives were changed. Many turned to Christ. But that way of evangelism has become less and less effective, even with training. "Christians do need training to share Christ cogently and confidently," says Thom Rainer. "However, the trainees should be taught that their training will be most effective among persons with whom they have developed a relationship. In other words, evangelism training is in, but cold call evangelism is out."[3]

Love is spelled T.I.M.E. It takes time to know people, to develop a relationship. "We are not much concerned with people we do not know. The first step toward reaching people is to discover them and get to know them."[4] Walls begin to crumble and the Holy

Spirit is able to convict when loving relationships are nurtured over time.

Beverly is a relationship builder. I know; I'm married to her. Little did she know our coming to Liberty would provide her the most unique ministry of her life. As a deputy clerk in the Chancery Court, she ministers to people at divorce hearings, youth court cases, as well as commitments to mental facilities. Relationship building comes easy for her. Some people have entered our church because she took the time to get to know them.

Introduce Them To Jesus

At some point in any evangelism strategy a verbal witness must be made if a person is to receive Christ. All of us can name someone at a certain place who introduced us to Jesus. We reach the lost sheep just as we were reached — one at a time.

It is the 10 percent of soul winners we must mobilize to reach the lost sheep one at a time and introduce them to Jesus. A church of 300 has approximately thirty soul winners. Thirty soul winners developing relationships and winning one a month for a year is 360 people brought into God's kingdom. A church of 300 is now twice as large!

Where do we send them to find them? *Everywhere!* "Behind doors, behind labels, behind masks, and behind barriers," says Darrell Robinson.[5] Where we find them we love them. When we love them, we reach them.

A systematic way of keeping up with lost people must be put in place. I've chosen to identify the lost under Darrell Robinson's four places to find the lost — behind doors, behind labels, behind masks, and behind barriers. Once identified, I've asked one of our soul winners who was saved from behind one of these categories to take that person (more on "teaming" in the next chapter) on as an object of prayer and personal soul winning. Those we cannot immediately identify are given to someone who may know them. A monthly "reveal" meeting is planned to celebrate victories and to keep our "reveal-ators" accountable in revealing Christ to the lost.

John had been a Catholic all his life but had little to do with the church. His visits to the priest for confession came after wild nights of partying or after a moral indiscretion on rare occasions. His standard response when asked about his faith was, "I'm Catholic." He was hiding behind this religious label.

We assigned John to Bill. Bill, too, was a former Catholic concealed behind the Catholic label. Bill understood the emptiness John had and his need for Christ. After months of cultivating a relationship, Bill was able to lead John to Christ.

Preach Or Declare The Gospel

Matthew 10:7 challenges us to preach and declare the gospel. Conversion evangelism takes place when we preach to the unchurched, declare to the unconcerned, and proclaim to the motivated.

* Preach To The Unchurched

A common concern expressed by the unchurched is the complaint that sermons are boring or irrelevant. They are generally boring because of style of delivery and irrelevant because of the lack of common ground with the unchurched in the areas of need, hurt, and interest.

Dr. Bruce Wilkerson's comments on teaching with style are equally applicable to preaching with style. He basically says if you are teaching (preaching) the way that comes natural for you, you are probably boring every time. We must take into consideration the external behaviors of our voice, eyes, face, gesture, posture, appearance, and movement.[6] Certain buildings you walk into, you want to stop and say, "This building has style." When the lost hear our preaching, do they say, "This preacher has style"?

My 3/3/50 Church Growth Survey reveals some 38 percent of pastors (Southern Baptist) consider their preaching with style of little, none, or some importance. Of the 57 percent who considered it very important, 40 percent were from pastors of growing churches. Presbyterians had 77 percent who felt it was of some importance with 22 percent saying it was very important. Preaching with style

96

for Methodists revealed some importance at 60 percent and 40 percent, very important. It is unlikely for pastors to preach with style if they do not recognize its value.

When you consider that Americans cite the quality of sermons as extremely important when choosing a church, it would be wise to make improvements in this area.[7] More pastors need to raise the level of excellence in their preaching and begin to preach with style.

If we use the "language of Zion" and preach "Bible exposition," our saved members will find it stimulating. The lost, once the terms are defined, will come to an understanding. Rick Warren in *The Purpose Driven Church* says to reach the unchurched in your preaching you need to "adapt your style to your audience, make the Bible accessible to unbelievers, provide an outline with scriptures written out, and build momentum by preaching in a series."[8] My only difference with Rick here is that the Bible can be made accessible to both believers and non-believers in the same service.

Have you ever been in a building that was originally built for one profession but was now being used for something else? It doesn't always work with the new customers without some major renovations. Some of our preaching needs to be fine-tuned if the new customers or unbelievers are to engage our product.

* Declare To The Unconcerned

The worship service is an experience designed to declare to the unconcerned and proclaim to the motivated. When we announce to unconcerned church members God's mandate for his church, we are revealing to them a picture of the lost without Christ, a story of life with Christ, and an opportunity for seizing the moment — a spiritual world view. "Religious information that is conveyed without the benefit of an organizing framework and spiritual worldview results in intellectual confusion and behavioral paralysis."[9]

Every worship service should have some aspect of declaring to the unconcerned. This organized framework can be done through a variety of ways: drama, music, spoken word, signing, multi-media, preaching, testimony, and more.

My pastor uses masterfully the dramatic tones of his voice, silence, inanimate objects, and word pictures to stir our hearts to action. Our people leave energized to take the gospel to a lost world.

Moving the unconcerned to the involved means more people immersed in the doing of conversion evangelism through personal invitations or the sharing of their faith. It takes them from being passive to having a passion for the lost. They become motivated.

* Proclaim To The Motivated

People who have the motivation to reach the lost do not need to be inspired again. Growth in their walk is needed. "It is thrifty to prepare today," said Aesop, "for the wants of tomorrow."[10] The motivated of our congregations want to reach the lost today but the preparation of spiritual growth is essential to have mentors for those reached tomorrow.

Our senior adult ministry took on this challenge in recent years by providing "Senior Focus" classes on Monday mornings. We became aware many of our seniors had never progressed past spiritual infancy. The classes provided some in-depth Bible studies and other spiritual reflection to move them to a new level in their walk. As go our senior adults, so go other age groups.

Preaching to the believers who are motivated will require systematic preaching verse by verse through a book or books of the Bible. It should be done with the attitude of preaching "not to the rebellious but to those who have said yes to God and want to go forward."[11]

In construction, "what the engineer tells his work crews is not very important compared with what the crews do when they go back to erecting the building."[12] Your proclamation to the motivated will instill in them a beautiful vision of the finished dwelling. It will deepen their understanding of remaining spiritually ahead of those they win. A new believer can only grow to the point of maturity that his mentor has.

Minister Freely

Matthew 10:8b tells us, "Freely you have received, freely give" (NIV). Since the laity will be the force that reveals Jesus to the lost world, "there must be some time," says David Hocking, "when the leader shows the ones he works with that they are more important to him than the task that needs to be done."[13] We do that in times of crisis and in times of celebration. It's in those moments that relationships are sealed and ministry marching orders can be given. The result is the staff ministers to the church leadership who in turn assist in ministering to the laity. The laity takes the gospel to the lost and unchurched and ministers in Jesus' name.

Ministry, when given, is done so freely. The world is yet to see what God can do in a community when a church totally and completely gives unfettered in ministry in Jesus' name. Its end result is a changed world, the essence of conversion evangelism.

I am almost at the point with our senior adult choir that they are at my beck and call. With three years of developing relationships, I believe they would attempt to do anything I ask of them. Not because of me, but because of the life of Christ in me. They know I would never ask them to do anything that I didn't feel God wanted. The end result has been a freeing — an unencumbered army of senior ministers.

"Be Wise And Harmless"

The going, preaching, and ministering all have potential hazards. It's at this point we need to remember to "be as wise as a serpent and harmless as a dove" (Matthew 10:16).

We are wise when we observe the laws governing solicitation, and harmless by using a direct mailout. We are wise when we preach so that the lost's needs are met, and harmless when topics are biblically-addressed hurts and interest. We are wise when we keep accurate records of our giving, but harmless when we claim our deductions in keeping with the law.

A wise builder knows the boundary lines, the laws governing his construction, and the quality of the materials used. It would be wise of us to do the same in the church when we go, preach, and minister in Jesus' name.

Entering a maximum security prison with a gospel message was a risky venture with a group of teenagers. We knew the risks. We knew the dangers. Yet, we were wise when we dealt at length with the warden and chaplain many times over a period of several months. No stone was left unturned concerning our arrival, setup, and procedure. The end result was a harmless outing with dramatic consequences in the lives of the prisoners.

Look back at chapter 1 under the structure of baptism. What did your church score? Poor, fair, good, or excellent structure? If you scored good or below, proceed with this "Frame" development.

Conversion Evangelism Frame Development

1. Our church can go to the lost sheep by_____
   _____.

   Examples: Inviting people to church through using a flyer, card, or promotional item; love them into a relationship by picking an individual to get to know; identifying the lost, assigning soul winners to the lost; and holding "reveal" meetings.

2. Our church can preach or declare the gospel by_____
   _____.

   Examples: Changing our style; systematically improving our worship services.

3. Our church can declare to the unconcerned by_____
   _____.

   Examples: Drama; music; spoken word; signing; multimedia; preaching; testimony.

4. Our church can proclaim to the motivated by _____
   _____.

   Examples: Expository preaching; rallying around a central purpose.

5. Our church can minister freely by _____
   _____.

   Examples: Affirming church leaders; recognition banquets; celebrating victories; developing relationships.

100

6. Our church can be "wise and harmless" by _____
_____.
   Examples: Observing the laws of the land, keeping accurate records, leaving no stone unturned.

---

1. Gary McIntosh and Glen Martin, *Finding Them, Keeping Them* (Nashville, Tennessee: Broadman Press, 1992), p. 6.

2. Barna, *The Frog In The Kettle*, p. 137.

3. Rainer, *The Book Of Church Growth*, p. 222.

4. Robinson, *Total Church Life*, p. 138.

5. *Ibid.*

6. Dr. Bruce Wilkinson, *Teaching With Style (Video Series)* (Nashville, Tennessee: Walk Through The Bible Ministries, 1994).

7. "Beliefs, Caring Sermons Draw Churchgoers," Barna Research Group, www.messenger-inquirer.com, October 24, 1998.

8. Warren, *The Purpose Driven Church*, pp. 294-301.

9. Barna, *The Habits Of Highly Effective Churches*, p. 140.

10. *Of Eagles Wings, Encouraging Words For Daily Life* (Anderson, Indiana: Warner Press, February 7, 1991).

11. Carl F. George, *How To Break Growth Barriers* (Grand Rapids: Michigan, Baker Book House, 1995), p. 79.

12. *Ibid.*, paraphrase of a football illustration, p. 80.

13. David Hocking, *The Seven Laws Of Christian Leadership* (Ventura, California: Regal Books, 1991), p. 282.

Chapter Ten

Framing With Comprehension Evangelism

Comprehension Evangelism is the growth frame where the final objective is to develop in Christ. Its function is to edify believers, leading them to be freely given to believing what they are taught. The focus of comprehension evangelism to the faithful finds its finished work when the faithful are grown in their faith, finding fulfillment with rules and principles for following. The phrase, "teaching all nations in the Great Commission," is the biblical basis for this plank.

The strategy for bringing about Comprehension Evangelism in our churches will take the form of capturing the new convert for further growth by teaming new Christians with mature Christians, providing care by enrolling them in a new members' class, cradling them by accessing an "in touch" plan, cultivating the class spirit, and commissioning them to progress past spiritual infancy.

Capture By Teaming
On a recent tour to the Cayman Islands, I was intrigued to learn that scuba diving clubs will assign a diving student to an

103

experienced diver. They do this for the divers' protection and for learning purposes. It's not to capture the new divers' interest; they already have it. But keeping their interest happens by assuring that the first few diving adventures turn out positively.

With new Christians, dangers are everywhere. The potential for losing them is at its highest soon after conversion. An assigned mentor who is mature in his or her faith provides protection from hazards and is there to encourage the new converts in their Christian walk. To capture means to take captive. By teaming a mature Christian with a new Christian we are beginning the first step of taking captive the believer's interest, directions, and plans to follow Christ.

When asked in our 3/3/50 Church Growth Survey, "Does your church have any kind of teaming or big brother system where you put a new Christian with a more mature Christian so that they can be discipled and nurtured?" 91 percent of all the churches (Southern Baptist), 88 percent of Presbyterians, and 80 percent of United Methodist said no.[1] It is no wonder we see many new converts falling through the cracks and never returning to active church life.

We can avoid this by instituting this teaming concept where the mature Christian's responsibilities center on praying, planning, and protecting the new convert — where he or she prays for the new Christian on a daily basis, plans with the convert a system of ongoing spiritual growth, and protects in the choices and friends made by using the "in touch" plan (to be covered later).

Teaming works. Whether it is assigning prayer partners for a mission trip to New York or CARE volunteers to new converts, it keeps each partner grounded in the faith. It is hard to go far into sin when a partner is keeping you accountable. Our success with the 36 new Christians hinged on this aspect.

Care By Enrolling

Every time I begin a new class, I do so because I know deep down that the class offered will meet real needs. It's a way of showing we care.

"For a church of 200 in attendance," says Thom Rainer, "up to twelve people will simply walk away."[2] New Christians will be among those who walk unless we enroll them in a new member class. This class should be required in order to be a member. Rick Warren says, "If little is required to join, very little can be expected from your members later on."[3]

Surprisingly, 71 percent of Southern Baptist churches, according to our survey said they did not have a new members' training class or some other system of orienting new members to their church. Twenty percent of the growing churches concurred. Presbyterians fared much better with 33 percent saying no as did United Methodists with 40 percent.[4]

Though Presbyterians and United Methodists do a better job in offering such a class, it hasn't stemmed the tide of people leaving their denominations. It may be the class is lacking, or many others factors are having a greater impact on people's departure.

This class, when offered, should be at least five sessions long, one hour each over a period of five weeks. The sessions should include

- Salvation Experience,
- Shared Vision,
- Single Strategy,
- Service Expectations, and
- Service Options.

Again, our success in keeping kids after their salvation experience involved such a class. Though some still fell by the wayside, the majority matured in their faith.

Cradle By Accessing

Following the new members class, the mature Christian who has been teamed with the new Christian should begin to implement the "in touch" plan. This accessing involves "touch opportunities undergirding Christian health."

Touch opportunities may be in the form of a personal visit, a coffee break, telephone call, or moments at church. Each should include the following questions:

1. What's going on in your life today?

2. Where are you in your spiritual growth plan?

3. What fears are you experiencing along your journey?

4. How can I help you?

"In touch" opportunities should happen at least once weekly over a period of six months.

David had been a Christian for six weeks and had gone through our new members' class. Brian, his spiritual mentor, was just beginning his "in-touch" plan with David. Knowing David worked night shifts and slept during the day, Brian caught David before Sunday school.

Brian: "Dave, can I talk with you a minute?"

David: "Sure."

Brian: "I just wanted to see how things were with you. What's going on in your life today?"

David: "Oh, not much. Well, to be honest with you, I'm struggling with my daily walk with the Lord. One minute I seem to be doing fine, and the next I'm falling on my face. What do you do?"

Brian: "Dave, even as Christians we still fall from time to time, but the more I become like Jesus the less I fall. It helps me if I'm consistent with my daily quiet time with the Lord."

David: "I haven't been consistent lately."

Brian: "So that must be where you are at in your spiritual growth plan?"

David: "Yes. I am fellowshiping with God's people regularly, but reading and praying in the morning is not working for me. I keep falling asleep after working all night."

Brian: "Try in the afternoon before you go to work."

David: "That's a thought. I'll give it a try."

Brian: "What fears are you experiencing?"

David: "None just yet, but I'll sure call on you when I do."

Brian: "Well, is there anything else I can do to help you?"

David: "No, Brian, you've done plenty already. Just keep praying for me."

Brian: "You can count on it. God bless you today. See you next week."

Brian went on in the coming weeks to cradle David gently, to rock him spiritually to the place where his spirit was quietened and his fears relieved. For fears did come, and so did Brian, touching David's life so he was able to move toward spiritual maturity.

Cultivate By Class Spirit

Nothing can move a new class member toward spiritual maturity better than a contagious class spirit. It has been said that more is caught than taught. A class that has "class" seems to bestow its collective class euphoria onto its membership in such a way that its least mature member is soon making giant strides toward becoming like Christ. These classes generally lead all others in giving, ministry, witnessing, and leadership development.

Judy's class is one that flourishes. Being around her, you won't go long without noticing her vivacious spirit, her love for the Lord, and her desire to have the best for her class. That's why it is one of our largest classes.

How can we cultivate this kind of class spirit? I'm convinced through years of experience it happens when the right teacher teaches, the right style is used, the right relationships are developed, and the right attitude is portrayed.

* The Right Teacher Teaches

Class spirit always begins with the teacher. The spirit with which the teacher teaches sets the tone for each week's class experience. Thus, the need for finding the right teacher.

The search for the right teacher begins with a teacher who has the spiritual gift of teaching. Paul Enns says, "This gift is clearly evidenced in a person who has profound biblical and theological truths and communicates them in a lucid way so ordinary people can readily grasp them."[5] "Highly effective churches recruit individuals to teach based upon spiritual gifts and spiritual maturity."[6]

Once this body of gifted leaders is known, placement can happen based on their preferred choice, history of previous teaching if any, and influence on certain age groups.

*The Right Style Used

A spiritually-gifted teacher does not automatically teach with style, with class. A boring teacher can possess the gift of teaching. Teachers must be trained in teaching with style. Great teaching begins in the heart but it must be nurtured there for long-term effectiveness. It uses the teacher's body involving the implementing of seven personality intangibles: those of energy, variety, transparency, humor, emotion, creativity, and motivation. Dr. David Wilkerson's video seminar *Teaching With Style* covers these abstracts and provides the tools for productive teaching.[7]

*The Right Relationships Developed

Before a new class can move toward maturity, the class relationships must consist of close, loving camaraderie. This begins with the teacher. A teacher is well on the way to a growing class when his or her members respect the teacher. This implies knowing the teacher prior to acceptance and revering the teacher's spiritual maturity. As a teacher models class acceptance and provides times of fellowship, class relationships are nurtured and developed.

*The Right Attitude Portrayed

Attitudes that kill a class are those that infer, "I'm responsible to teach. You are responsible to come." There's a hint of truth to that statement but what comes across is, "I don't care." To cultivate the right kind of class spirit we must possess a "holy imagination" of what God can lead a person to become.[8] This kind of attitude is contagious because it is God-initiated in the heart of the believer.

*Commission By Progression

The reason for progressing new believers past spiritual infancy is so that they can be commissioned to reach other new believers for Christ. Once they reach them, then they can assist them through the process of capturing, caring, cradling, cultivating, and commissioning.

Look back at chapter 1 under the structure of teaching. What did your church score? Poor, good, or excellent in teaching? If you scored good or below, proceed with this "Frame" development.

Comprehension Evangelism "Frame" Development

1. Our church can capture new converts for further growth by

_____

_____.

    Examples: Teaming new Christians with a mature Christian; making first class experience positive; implementing prayer plan for new believer; developing a system of ongoing spiritual growth, use an "in-touch" plan.

2. Our church can provide care for new members by _____

_____.

    Examples: Enrolling them in a new members' class; visiting in the home soon after joining; helping establish a circle of friends.

3. Our church can cradle new members with touch opportunities by _____

_____.

    Examples: Personal visits; using coffee breaks; telephone calls; breaks at church; implementing the "in-touch" plan.

4. Our church can cultivate the class spirit by _____

_____.

    Examples: Enlisting the right teacher; developing the right style; choosing teachers who are respected; instilling the right attitude.

5. Our church can commission others by _____

_____.

    Examples: Taking each through the process of capturing, caring, cradling, and cultivating; being there in times of crisis and celebration; modeling process by leadership.

1. 3/3/50 Church Growth Survey by author.

2. Rainer, *The Book Of Church Growth*, p. 284.

3. Warren, *The Purpose Driven Church*, p. 315.

4. 3/3/50 Church Growth Survey by author.

5. Paul Enns, *The Moody Handbook Of Theology* (Chicago, Illinois: Moody Press, 1989), p. 275.

6. Barna, *The Habits Of Highly Effective Churches*, p. 137.

7. Dr. Bruce Wilkerson, *Teaching With Style (Video Seminar)*, Walk Through The Bible Ministries, 1994. This resource can be purchased through LifeWay Christian Resources of the Southern Baptist Convention.

8. George, *How To Break Growth Barriers*, p. 122.

Chapter Eleven

Framing With Confirmation Evangelism

The new believer is now firmly planted in the class. Now we must provide the spiritual nourishment that will lead him in a systematic way in growth. These spiritual growth prerequisites come in the areas of Bible study, prayer, worship, and the sharing of one's faith. The result is an evangelism that began with a community awareness event that is now confirmed and strengthened through this plank.

* Strengthened Through Bible Study

Confirmation evangelism involves a systematic way of Bible study that strengthens and matures class members. "Only through study can we see God's direction for our lives," say Gary McIntosh and Glenn Martin, "and become motivated to walk in the steps that He has laid before us."[1]

My successes at growing children, teens, and adults through Bible study came because I sought to lead them to know God, hear God, think like God, and obey God. Regardless of the curriculum used, this process developed mature saints by immersing people in his Word.

No retreat needs to be held without at least five hours of intense Bible study. No discipleship plan needs to be undertaken without some emphasis on Scripture memory.

Nurturing the teens in central Mississippi involved a strong emphasis in Sunday school. The adults in south Mississippi encountered God's Word at greater depths with a focus in Discipleship Training on Sunday nights. The senior adults are experiencing greater insights through our Senior Focus classes.

* Strengthened Through Prayer

"In an age in which the stakes are growing ever higher in the daily spiritual battles of all people," says George Barna, "prayer is indisputably one of the greatest and most under-utilized weapons we have at our disposal."[2] "In user friendly churches, prayer was one of the foundation stones of ministry. The congregation was exposed to biblical teaching about the role of prayer in the Christian life. Church leaders modeled prayer as normal and significant behavior in all aspects of the Christian life. These churches had learned to celebrate the fruits of prayer. The congregation was held accountable for prayer."[3]

We bring the strength of prayer to our membership when we expose the biblical truths on prayer, set an example through leadership, esteem the fruits of prayer, and expect prayer from our members' lives.

The following chart gives some practical ways of introducing the strength of prayer to our memberships:

Exposure	Example	Esteem	Expectation
1. Preaching	1. Public	1. Testimonies	1. Request Prayer
2. Teaching	2. Private/ Public	2. Prayers Of Praise	2. Call On Them

3. Singing Prayers In Quiet Time	3. Singing Worship	3. Praise And Worship	3. True
4. Prayer Retreat	4. Staff Active In Prayer Ministry	4. Provide Opportunities	
5. Make available Prayer Library.			

Our 3/3/50 Church Growth Survey revealed prayer ministries are alive and well. Southern Baptists use a wide variety of prayer mechanisms while 77 percent of Presbyterians use prayer chains, 33 percent have prayer ministries, and 33 percent men's prayer groups. United Methodists showed 80 percent using prayer chains, 80 percent having prayer ministries, and 60 percent offering ladies' prayer groups. Though having prayer ministries doesn't guarantee a growing church, it is a significant factor listed among churches that are growing.

Everywhere I've gone to serve, God has had me right in the middle of the prayer ministry — as I should be. I have been instrumental in developing prayer warriors. The thirteen music groups with 320 musicians has a close connection to my deep involvement in prayer ministry.

* Strengthen Through Worship

Worship is the place where the overflow of the heart is allowed to express itself. Whether it is private worship or corporate, it should be participatory, praise-oriented, and perfected.

Worship that is participatory provides every opportunity for the membership to be involved. Gary McIntosh says to "build in ways for people to participate by allowing singing, clapping, shaking hands, praying, hugging, talking, laughing, crying, and other ways that would be acceptable to your worshipers."[4]

More participation is possible when the worship leaders are sensitive to the preferred music style of the community and prior worship traditions. This is especially true for Boomers and Busters. "For both Busters and Boomers, music is almost sacred; they crave musical expression but possess very little tolerance for music they cannot comprehend or that seems antiquated."[5]

Worship that is praise-oriented speaks directly to God the Father. It seeks to lift up Christ so that all men may be drawn unto him. It uses the name of Jesus throughout the service. (How many times in your services of worship is the name of Jesus mentioned?) "Worship is directed toward God," says Robert Bailey, "not any person or organization. We honor God. We praise God. We adore God. We obey God. We praise God above all the earth."[6]

Worship that is perfected is worship that uses all the senses. It magnifies beauty through sight and sound. It inspires commitment through the symbolic touching of the heart. It delights through the tasting of the goodness of the Lord (Psalm 34:8).

Worship that is perfected is worship that is of the finest quality. Quality on the inside and the outside of each leader and worshiper is demanded. Hence, the need for times of confession. A fine piece of music done with excellence by the choir, but with sin in the heart, is of no value. A clean heart with quality singing is our goal. We can have both. "The concept of quality," says George Barna, "seemed to involve five aspects of the healthy churches I studied: integrity, excellence in effort, consistency, credibility, and reliability."[7]

Early in my ministry, I lost sight of how important worship was to the health of the church. With a rekindled desire to present the best of my offerings to God, I've now made a conscious effort towards excellence. Quality worship experiences have followed. The church can't help but flourish when God knows we've given 110 percent of our best. God honors such selfless giving when done to honor him.

* Strengthened Through Fellowship

Fellowship was extensively addressed in chapter 6 under the anchors of disciple making so will not spend much time here. Suffice it to say that fellowship is the mortar that makes all these prerequisites come together to produce spiritual growth. Bible study without it becomes a chore to endure. Prayer in the absence of fellowship becomes a ritual of words with no power. Worship without fellowship becomes a contradiction in terms. Fellowship happens when we lead our people to embrace each other around a central purpose for being together.

The youth group I had in my hometown demonstrated this truth. What happened there still wells up inside me when I consider how God multiplied that group before my eyes. The Bible studies, retreats, tours, mission trips, all revolved around a central purpose — "reaching their peers for Christ." The reality of that happening rested on the deep fellowship we had with God and each other.

* Strengthened Through Sharing One's Faith

The ultimate climax of the spiritual growth prerequisites is when new believers have grown to the place where they can now be commissioned to share their faith. They are strengthened by this sharing because it solidifies and verifies in one's mind their own faith. Witnessing is the last bastion of truth that most Christians ever get around to doing. When they do, a great sense of joy overcomes them because they know they are doing what the Master said.

A group of a dozen teenagers attended a WOW (Win Our World) Weekend a number of years ago. As youth minister, I had brought in another youth leader from Alabama to facilitate this training. A Friday night and a Saturday morning session were provided to train them in using a tract in sharing the gospel. Saturday afternoon was used as a time to go to visit some lost teenagers identified by a list we had prepared and present a tract to them.

I'll never forget the overwhelming joy on the faces of those youth after having won some of their friends to the Lord. For several it was the first time they had shared their faith.

Look back at chapter 6 under the covering (roof) of discipleship. What did your church score? If you scored good or below, proceed with the following "Frame" development.

Confirmation Evangelism Frame Development

1. Our church can strengthen the spiritual growth prerequisite of Bible study _____

    _____.

    Examples: By helping age groups know, hear, think like, and obey God; by enlisting gifted teachers.

2. Our church can strengthen the spiritual growth prerequisite of prayer by _____

    _____.

    Examples: Exposing congregation to teachings on prayer; leaders setting an example; esteeming the fruits of prayer, expecting prayer from their lives; establishing a prayer ministry.

3. Our church can strengthen the spiritual growth prerequisite of worship by _____

    _____.

    Examples: Designing ways people can participate; making worship praise-oriented (using the name of Jesus); perfecting it through quality inside and out.

4. Our church can strengthen the spiritual growth prerequisite of fellowship by _____

    _____.

    Examples: Periodic fellowships; sharing opportunities; having small groups (clusters) testimonies.

5. Our church can strengthen the spiritual growth prerequisite of sharing one's faith by _____

    _____.

    Examples: Providing witness training, witness opportunities; CWT; Evangelism Explosion, People Sharing Jesus; WOW (Win Our World) Weekend.

We have evaluated our present church structure through the building of the house. Plans have been suggested for designing a blueprint in framing the work to be done using the areas of community awareness, conversion, comprehension, and confirmation evangelism. It has been our guide to reaching and assimilating people. Now comes the task of tailoring your church growth frame so that your church can begin or continue to grow — built by the Owner's design.

---

1. McIntosh and Martin, *Finding Them, Keeping Them*, p. 98.

2. Barna, *Successful Churches: What They Have In Common*, p. 15.

3. Barna, *User Friendly Churches*, p. 112.

4. Gary McIntosh, *The Exodus Principle* (Nashville, Tennessee: Broadman and Holman, 1995), pp. 93-94.

5. Barna, *The Habits Of Highly Effective Churches*, p. 102.

6. Robert W. Bailey, *New Ways In Christian Worship* (Nashville, Tennessee: Broadman Press, 1981), p. 17.

7. Barna, *User Friendly Churches*, p. 62.

Chapter Twelve

What Now?

We have examined "framing the work" and have developed the four planks of evangelism. Now it's time for us to put the structures we've discovered into a tailored evangelism frame for your church.

Look back at chapter 4, chapter 5, and chapter 6 to determine if you scored your foundation, outreach, baptism, and teaching checklist as excellent. If you did, there is no need to work on improving those growth frames. If the foundation checklist showed less than excellent, work on shoring it up first by moving to the following growth frames. Your score on the teaching checklist should apply to both the comprehension and confirmation growth frames.

First, on the blank frames, (figure F1), list present ministries your church has that fit the evangelism planks of community awareness (going), conversion (baptism), comprehension (teaching), and confirmation (discipleship). For example, Sunday school would go with the comprehension frame. A ministry may appear in more than one evangelism frame based on the nature of the ministry; for example, Sunday school may also fit the conversion frame. Allow fifteen minutes for this present ministry framing.

Framing The Work
Present Ministries

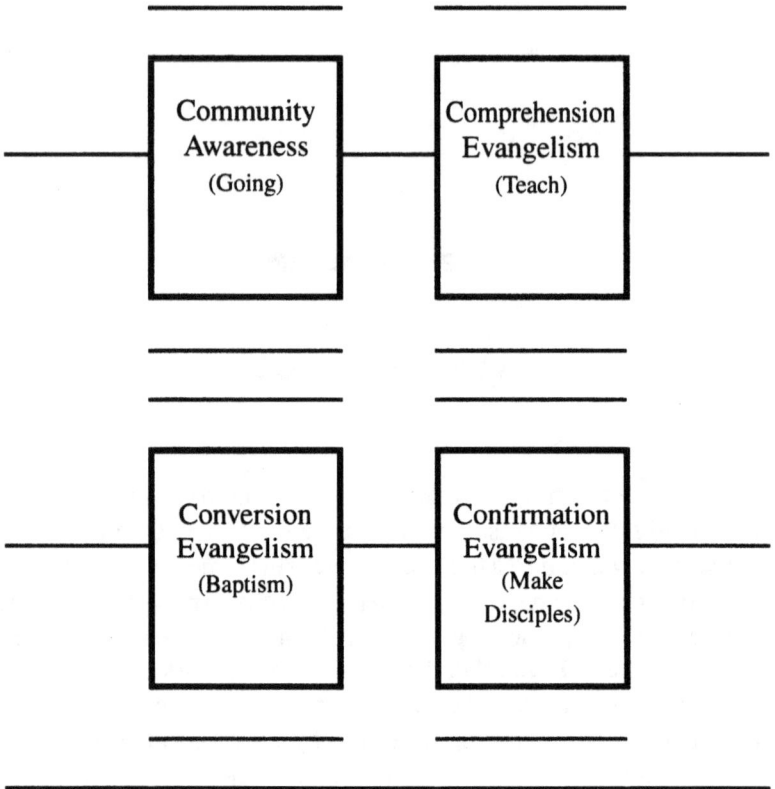

Community
Awareness
(Going)

Comprehension
Evangelism
(Teach)

Conversion
Evangelism
(Baptism)

Confirmation
Evangelism
(Make
Disciples)

Figure F1

Now that you've listed all of your present ministries, go back and number each one, 1 through 4, with 1 being the ministry that best fulfills the evangelism frame. If you have more ministries than lines given to each evangelism frame, add additional lines. If you have just one or two ministries in each frame, that's all right. Also, you can have more than one of each number in a frame. For example, you may put a 1 by Sunday school and a home Bible study in the comprehension frame if you feel both equally fulfill that evangelism frame the best. Allow ten minutes to accomplish this ministry effectiveness analysis.

Now transfer all the ministries that you have placed a 1 or 2 beside to the Present and Needed Ministries chart, (figure F2). Eliminate all ministries you have placed a 3 or 4 beside, unless you feel that a particular ministry is a valid ministry but needs new life

Framing The Work
Present And Needed Ministries

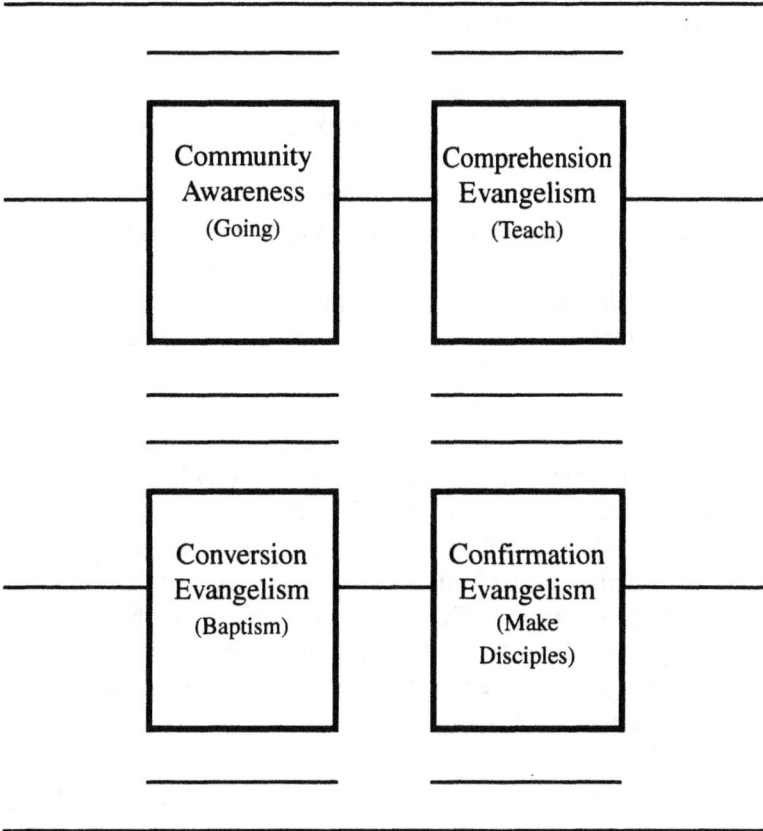

Community Awareness (Going)	Comprehension Evangelism (Teach)
Conversion Evangelism (Baptism)	Confirmation Evangelism (Make Disciples)

Figure F2

breathed into it. Be sure you are not falling prey to one of the temptations Lyle Schaller writes[1] about why churches do not move off plateau in size: an unwillingness to change, attractiveness of the *status quo*, or the reluctance to pay the price of change. If you have consistently tried to make a ministry work and it hasn't, let it go. God is not blessing it.

You probably have some blanks left at each evangelism frame. Use the ministry suggestions from chapters 8 through 11 or come up with some of your own to place in each. This time of ministry transfer should take about twenty minutes.

To evaluate further your ministry balance, use the scoring chart to determine your church score.

Scoring Chart
Frame The Work

Frame	Points
Community Awareness	10 points (for each ministry)
Conversion	8 points (for each ministry)
Comprehension	6 points (for each ministry)
Confirmation	3 points (for each ministry)

Scoring

If a balance is achieved in all four evangelism frames, then the following scoring is true: Small Church = 36-54 Excellent; 18-35 Good but could be improved; 3-17 Poor balance; Medium Sized Church = 79-118 Excellent; 40-78 Good but could be improved; 1-39 Poor balance; Large Church = 108-162 Excellent; 54-107 Good but could be improved; 27-53 Poor balance; Super Church = 139-208 Excellent; 69-138 Good but could be improved; 27-68 Poor balance; Mega Church = 175-262 Excellent; 87-174 Good but could be improved; 27-86 Poor balance.

Note: If your present frame is not balanced, then look for ministries to achieve balance or drop ministries from evangelism frames that are ministry saturated. Too many ministries and you are overstructured; too few, understructured. This scoring chart is based on a mega church, 3,000-6,000 in attendance; super church, 1,000-3,000; large church, 200-1,000 medium size church, 50-200; small church, less than 50. A home group, from 5 to 35 in attendance, can reduce each frame to a minimum of one ministry in each. Its total score would be compared to a 27 total. The large, super, and mega churches add 8 different ministries, 2 in each frame; hence, a large church would have 24 ministries on the average; super church, 32; mega church, as many as 40. Scoring would be based on a 162 point total for a large church; 208 points for a super church; and 262 points for a mega church. Divide these scorings by three to determine excellent, good, or poor strategy.

Once completed, you will have a tailored plan for growth that is balanced. Now get started! Your church is waiting to implement these structures — a task they've longed to do. Follow the Owner's design.

---

1. Schaller, *44 Steps Up Off The Plateau*, pp. 57, 58, and 61.

Supporting Documents

Church Growth Survey

Completed: 1999/2000

Participants:
50 Churches, 3 Baptist Associations, 3 Denominations

1. Does your church have a long range plan in place?
   SBC - 65% no, 34% yes
   UMC - 60% no, 40% yes
   PUSA - 77% no, 22% yes

   If yes, is it written in the form of a vision for your church?
   SBC - 11%
   UMC - 40%
   PUSA - 11%

2. Do most of your members know their spiritual gifts?
   SBC - 31% yes, 65% no, 2.8% I don't know
   UMC - 20% yes, 80% no
   PUSA - 11% yes, 89% no

   If yes, does your church have a system of placing people according to their gifts?
   SBC - 20%
   UMC - 20%
   PUSA - 11%

3. Can your church now and has it in the past been able to discern truth in times of crisis?
   SBC - 74% yes, 26% no
   UMC - 40% yes, 20% no, 40% no response or not sure
   PUSA - 66% yes, 33% no

If yes, describe one such crisis and how truth was discerned.

* Embezzlement by secretary taught us to do justice and love mercy
* Modernist domination of former denomination; truth discerned through preaching of Scripture, teaching of confessional documents
* Conflict between session and deacons and congregation; sought counsel and prayed. The two elders resigned
* From the Bible
* Working to overcome crisis of racial tension and problems in the community
* Twenty years ago, when a former pastor admitted he was struggling with sexual identity, the congregation did not call for his removal. He later resigned. Five years ago, we made a decision to be in ministry to the local community — formally inviting blacks to join our fellowship
* Church split, 1950s; perseverance, continues a good relationship with the sister church that was created
* Concern over new missions opportunities resulted in a strengthened attitude about missions
* Flood victims were helped with food, clothes, money, etc.
* During remodeling of fellowship hall — many ideas; one settled on — not by controlling members
* Truth of God's Word with former pastor
* A staff member with a sexual problem. Truth discerned through much prayer and interviews with those involved
* To rebuild or remodel
* Sudden death of a central member
* Church burned — rebuilt and paid in full — completion with money left over
* Investigation held and brought to floor of the church
* Through the birth of a newborn baby
* Financial hardship brought on controversy — prayed through the situation — we realized we had overburdened our budget
* A devil worshiper disrupted service. We had him arrested and then led him to Christ

* With regard to whether we should be open to selling property at present location
* Murder of a lady member of the church — murder of teenager in the church by another

4. Is your church plateau, declining, or growing?
    SBC - 57% growing, 34% declining, 0.8% plateaued
    UMC - 80% growing, 0% declining, 20% plateaued
    PUSA - 22% growing, 33% declining, 44% plateaued

5. Does your church offer evangelism training throughout the year?
    SBC - 42% yes, 57% no
    UMC - 20% yes, 80% no
    PUSA - 0% yes, 100% no

6. On a scale of 1-10, how evangelistic do you see your church?
    SBC - 3.7 average
    UMC - 5.1 average
    PUSA - 3.5 average

7. Does your church have a "new member" class or some other system of orienting new members to the church?
    SBC - 28% yes, 72% no
    UMC - 40% yes, 40 % no, 20% no response
    PUSA - 66% yes, 33% no

If yes, what do you have?
* Membership training class
* A program of linking them with support and ministry groups as soon as possible after joining
* We attempt to do a new member training as needed
* Catechism Training
* Periodic 13-week orientation class in Sunday school
* A program designed by the pastor — 8-12 weeks in length
* Teach doctrines and government in our church
* Introductory class and follow-up (6 weeks and 13 weeks)

* Survival Kits
* In Sunday school we have a "Taking The Next Step" class
* Seven Steps booklet for all new members plus class and fellowship
* One on one
* Beginning Steps — 7 Day Growth Guide For New Believers — Home Mission Board Publication
* What Baptist Believe, etc. Doctrines
    SBC - Most Common (Survival Kits)
    UMC - Most Common (New Members Class)
    PUSA - Most Common (Catechism Training)

8. Does your church take great care in making sure new converts understand the demands of discipleship?
    SBC - 60% yes, 34% no, 3% no response
    UMC - 60% yes, 40% no
    PUSA - 66% yes, 34% no

9. How would you describe the quality of teaching in your church?
    SBC - 20% excellent, 66% good, 11% fair, 3% no response
    UMC - 40% excellent, 40% good, 20% fair
    PUSA - 0% excellent, 77% good, 11% fair, 12% no response

10. Has your church adopted in business a church mission statement?
    SBC - 51% yes, 49% no
    UMC - 100% yes
    PUSA - 66% yes, 34% no

11. Does your church have any kind of accountability built into it related to attendance, discipline, or discipleship?
    SBC - 83% no, 11% yes, 6% no response
    UMC - 100% no
    PUSA - 55% yes, 45% no

12. What area(s) of church life does your church look for growth to occur? (i.e., Sunday school, revivals, personal soul winning, etc.)

> SBC - 41% Sunday school, 25% revivals, 25% personal soul winning, 9% other
>
> UMC - 40% Sunday school, 20% morning worship, 20% children's ministries, 20% personal witness
>
> PUSA - 20% worship, 20% Sunday school, 10% evangelism, 20% kindergarten/playschool, 30% other

13. Is your church over-structured (a lot going on but little results), under-structured (little happening with complaints your church is not offering enough), structured wrong (programmatic but not evangelistic), or structured just right (the right mix of programs that have an evangelistic thrust)?

> SBC - 9% over-structured, 23% under-structured, 31% structured wrong, 31% structured just right, 6% no response
>
> UMC - 0% over-structured, 20% under-structured, 20% structured wrong, 40% structured just right, 20% no response
>
> PUSA - 22% over-structured, 44% under-structured, 22% structured wrong, 11% structured just right

14. Does your church have trouble finding people to fill leadership positions?

> SBC - 49% yes, 49% no, 2% no response
>
> UMC - 40% yes, 60% no
>
> PUSA - 77% yes, 23% no

15. How aware is your community of what your church has to offer its citizens?

> SBC - 6% it's not, 17% little aware, 63% some aware, 11% lot aware
>
> UMC - 0% it's not, 60% little aware, 40% some aware, 0% lot aware
>
> PUSA - 11% it's not, 33% little aware, 55% some aware, 0% lot aware

16. Does your church have any kind of "teaming" or big brother system where you put a new Christian with a mature Christian so they can be discipled and nurtured?

> SBC - 9% yes, 91% no
> UMC - 20% yes, 80% no
> PUSA - 11% yes, 89% no

17. How important do you consider style in your preaching? (manner, way, and the how of delivery)

> SBC - 3% no importance, 9% little importance, 26% some importance, 57% very important
> UMC - 0% no importance, 60% little importance, 40% some importance, 0% very important
> PUSA - 0% no importance, 0% little importance, 77% some importance, 23% very important

18. How important is prayer in your church? Check those that apply. Your church has:

> SBC - (multiple responses) 42% prayer chains, 40% prayer ministry, 20% times of prayer and fasting, 25% cottage prayer meetings, 17% prayer room, 17% Sunday school prayer leaders, 22% men's prayer group, 37% ladies' prayer group, 11% other
> UMC - (multiple responses) 80% prayer chains, 80% prayer ministry, 20% cottage prayer meetings, 40% men's prayer group, 60% ladies' prayer group, 20% prayer room, 20% other
> PUSA - (multiple responses) 77% prayer chains, 22% Wednesday prayer, 33% prayer ministry, 33% men's prayer group, 11% ladies' prayer group, 11% elder prayer, 11% other.